HEARST'S DREAM

HEARST'S DREAM

by

Taylor Coffman

ILLUSTRATED BY
CHARLES COLLINS

EZ NATURE BOOKS · SAN LUIS OBISPO · 1989

I want to thank ARA Leisure Services, Inc., publishers of *Hearst Castle: The Story of William Randolph Hearst and San Simeon,* for allowing me to use portions of the text I wrote for that book, which came out in 1985 and remains in print. I have drawn upon *Hearst Castle* throughout the writing of this new book, although much of the previous text I have used appears here in a revised and reorganized form. In addition, *Hearst's Dream* contains extensive portions I have written expressly for it. I also want to thank John Porter, my editor for many years, whose help was again indispensable.   —T.C.

The drawings in *Hearst's Dream* range from adaptations of photographs and other images in the public domain to original compositions of my own. Among the books I consulted, Jo Mora's *Californios,* Oscar Lewis's *Fabulous San Simeon,* and Emil White's *Full Color Guide to the Hearst Castle* were especially helpful. I want to thank the *Sun-Bulletin* (Morro Bay) for letting me work from Toni Booth's photograph of Pete Sebastian that appeared in its issue of April 12, 1984. I also want to thank the Loorz family for letting me work from the photograph of George Loorz in its possession.   —C.C.

FRONTISPIECE: *Entrance to Casa Grande, the main building at La Cuesta Encantada*

ISBN 0-945092-07-5

Design and typography by Jim Cook/Santa Barbara

Published by EZ Nature Books
Post Office Box 4206
San Luis Obispo, California

Contents

Illustrations

PROLOGUE:
San Simeon

THE NAME *San Simeon* is identified far and wide with William Randolph Hearst's palatial home, an architectural wonder usually called Hearst Castle even though its real name is La Cuesta Encantada, or, to translate from Hearst's whimsical Spanish, The Enchanted Hill. *San Simeon,* however, also applies to a point jutting into the Pacific, to a creek and its backcountry reaches, to an old mission rancho and a Mexican land grant, to a picturesque nineteenth-century village—in other words, to an area, a micro-region, a little corner of California.

Extending east along San Simeon Creek, continuing north past Rocky Butte and Pine Mountain, and curving west to San Carpoforo Creek and the beginning of the Big Sur country is the crescent of mountain and foothill, coastal plain and shore-line known as San Simeon. Geographically isolated except where it gives way to the forested hills of Cambria, San Simeon is a land apart, guarded by the Coast Range on one side and the Pacific Ocean on the other. At a point almost exactly in its center lies La Cuesta Encantada, the crown jewel of Hearst's principality, the foremost manifestation of Hearst's dream. A finer arrangement of man-made and natural elements would be hard to find.

San Simeon's early heritage is Spanish-Mexican and, earlier still, Chumash, though only the most limited traces of aboriginal occupation survive. The Chumash can be remembered at least by the names they gave to their settlements. Recorded in mission annals, the names are exotic, often lyrical—names like Tissimassu, Zay, Tsetacol, Stajahuayo, and Zaha Saltanel. Except for Chinese mariners who may have sailed past these shores in the dim antiquity before the Spaniards appeared— the possibility is enticing, however remote—none but the Chumash and other native peoples knew San Simeon for thousands of years. Then came Juan Rodriguez Cabrillo, who plied the coast late in 1542 but who dropped anchor nowhere in the area—despite an oft-repeated account that he moored in San Simeon Bay. Cabrillo named the coastwise mountains in this vicinity the *Sierras de San Martin* and those closer to Big Sur and Monterey the *Sierras Nevadas.* But Cabrillo's two names were destined to be replaced by a single one, the *Sierra de Santa Lucia,* which Sebastian Vizcaino bestowed on the northern part of the Santa Lucia Range during his voyage in 1602 and which the Portola expedition adopted for the entire range during its trek in 1769.

The diaries from that first Portola expedition provide the earliest detailed descriptions of the San Simeon coast and have

The San Simeon area was long thought to have fallen entirely within the domain of the Salinan peoples. More recent research has moved the Chumash-Salinan boundary northward from Cayucos to Ragged Point or Salmon Creek on the lower Big Sur coast. Of the Chumash place names recorded for the area, Zaha Saltanel *equates roughly with Cambria,* Stajahuayo *with San Simeon Creek,* Tissimassu *with San Simeon Bay,* Zay *with Arroyo de la Cruz, and* Tsetacol *with San Carpoforo Creek.*

II

been widely quoted, especially Father Juan Crespi's.* Too often, though, a far more vivid description of San Simeon during the late 1700s has been overlooked, the account left by George Vancouver, an Englishman who sailed south past the area in 1793:

"About nine o'clock we passed a low projecting point [Point Piedras Blancas], off which lie, at a small distance, two or three rugged detached rocks; the outermost is situated in latitude 35′ 42″, longitude 239′ 6″; from whence the line of the coast, for a short distance, inclines a few degrees more to the eastward; the mountains fall further back from the water-side, and the intermediate country appeared to be a plain, or to rise with a very gradual ascent, for the space of about four leagues along the coast. This land was tolerably well wooded, even close down to the shore; and by the assistance of our glasses some of the trees were seen to be very large, with spreading branches; and being for the greater part distributed in detached clumps, produced a very pleasing effect, and a prospect more fertile than we had lately been accustomed to behold."

Vancouver also described the native inhabitants in a passage providing much food for ethnographical thought:

"This difference in the appearance of the country was not confined to inanimate nature, for its inhabitants seemed to benefit by its superior productions, as we soon discovered a canoe approaching us, of a construction I little expected to have met with. Instead of its being composed of straw like those we had seen on our first visit to port San Francisco, it was neatly formed of wood, much after the Nootka [Vancouver Island] fashion, and was navigated with great adroitness by four of the natives of the country. Their paddles were about ten feet long, with a blade at each end; these they handled with much dexterity either intirely [sic] on one side,

---

*For a detailed account of the first of the two Portola expeditions through the San Simeon area see Paul Squibb, ed., *Captain Portola in San Luis Obispo County in 1769* (Morro Bay: Tabula Rasa Press, 1984; San Luis Obispo County Heritage Series 1).

or alternately on each side of their canoe. The exertions to reach us were very great, but as we were favored with a fresh gale, with all sails set, they were not able to come up with us; and I regretted that I could not afford some leisure for a better acquaintance with these people, who seemed, by the ingenuity displayed in their canoe, to differ very materially from those insensible beings we had met in the neighbourhood of San Francisco and Monterey."

By the end of that same day in 1793 Vancouver had sailed as far as the headland he named Point Sal. The next day he named another headland Point Arguello—a headland that on clear days can be seen in the blue distance, eighty miles south, from William Randolph Hearst's Enchanted Hill.

Ironically, the origin of the name *San Simeon*—the name that speaks for what Hearst built as well as for an entire locality—has yet to be definitively traced. The name has traditionally been associated with Mission San Miguel Arcangel, which was founded in 1797, although Mission San Luis Obispo is now known to have been baptizing Indians from the San Simeon area as early as the 1770s. Mission San Miguel, at any rate, had reached far to the west by about 1805 to embrace the land surrounding the Chumash village of Stajahuayo, near the mouth of San Simeon Creek; and in 1810, according to the mission annals, San Miguel built an adobe there. Two years later, on July 8, 1812, an old Chumash woman was baptized at *El Rancho de San Simeon*. This occurrence of the name is apparently the earliest. The next occurrence in the annals dates from early in 1819, when Father Antonio Rodriguez of Mission San Luis Obispo mentioned the "punta del rancho de S. Simeon" in two letters to the governor of Spanish California. (The apparent reference to San Simeon Point suggests that the name had already become identified with more than the mission rancho—or perhaps even that the name had originally been applied to the point itself.) In 1827 Father Juan Cabot of Mission San Miguel, in his report to the governor of what was by then Mexican California, referred to the coastal rancho simply as *San Simeon*. Not until 1830 did the full name *Rancho de San Simeon en la Playa* appear in the annals of San Miguel.

A related question is *which* of numerous Saint Simeons the name commemorates. Nellie Van de Grift Sanchez offered two possibilities in her *Spanish and Indian Place Names of California*, the apostle Simon (or Simeon, as he has sometimes been called) and the fifth-century Simeon Stylites the Elder. Phil Townsend Hanna adopted the latter possibility in his *Dictionary of California Land Names*. But Henry Raup Wagner, in citing a feast day of February 18 in his article "Saints' Names in California," indicated a third possibility, the Simeon who was martyred about the year 107 under the Roman emperor Trajan. That these and other discrepancies still exist makes the study of *San Simeon* a challenging exercise in the pursuit of local history.

By the time Mission San Miguel established its San Simeon rancho, neighboring Mission San Antonio de Padua, which Father Junipero Serra founded soon after the Portola expeditions of 1769 and 1770, had been using the upper part of the San Simeon coast for summer pasturage for many years. Both missions may well have regarded the coast as more than good grazing land. San Simeon Bay, for instance, was the only

Of California's eventual twenty-one missions, San Miguel Arcangel was one of four founded in 1797 to fill gaps in the chain. By about 1805 Mission San Miguel was able to assume Mission San Luis Obispo's proselytizing and other work in the far-removed San Simeon area. A narrow trail from San Miguel to San Simeon crossed the Santa Lucia Range south of Pine Mountain and Rocky Butte. But the heavy carretas (oxcarts) that sometimes attempted the trip undoubtedly had to go the long way around—probably southwest by way of Old Creek to Cayucos and then up the coast through Rancho San Geronimo and Rancho Santa Rosa.

reliable anchorage for miles in either direction. During the first two decades of the 1800s—the final years of Spanish rule in California—the bay probably provided occasional refuge for whalers, fur traders, and other mariners; it may also have provided a commercial port of call. Commerce was rigidly controlled during the Spanish regime—in theory at least—but the lack of supplies from Mexico prompted the California missions to trade increasingly with foreign vessels. The traffic in sea otter pelts, cattle hides, tallow, and other goods not only provided the missions with many necessities but also contributed to the feudalistic prosperity they enjoyed.

Did Mission San Miguel and Mission San Antonio actually trade through San Simeon Bay, either during the restrictive Spanish regime or during the more accommodating Mexican one? Geneva Hamilton, in *Where the Highway Ends,* believes they did, especially Mission San Miguel. From 1823 to 1826, for example, when the English hide-and-tallow traders McCulloch, Hartnell and Company had an exclusive contract with the California missions, San Luis Obispo Bay was designated as the collecting point for San Miguel's products. San Miguel may have found it expedient at the same time, as Hamilton believes, to trade in defiance of the contract through its own backyard port of San Simeon. No figures appear to exist for livestock on the San Simeon rancho during the contract period, but as soon thereafter as 1827 Father Juan Cabot could report 800 cattle for San Simeon alone—more than a third of San Miguel's total holdings of 2,130 head that year.

An earlier writer on the subject of coastal trade, Edith Buckland Webb, implied in her *Indian Life at the Old Missions* that Mission San Antonio delivered its hides and tallow to San Simeon. (Monterey, however, was designated as San Antonio's collecting point, at least during the McCulloch, Hartnell contract.) On the other hand, Alfred Robinson of Bryant, Sturgis and Company, the Boston hide-and-tallow traders, referred to San Simeon in *Life in California* as "a beautiful little bay" but one that was "seldom visited by navigators"—this in the context of 1830. He also likened Mission San Miguel to Mission San Antonio in its possession of "few resources, owing to its distance from the sea-coast, and the moderate extent of its domains." It seems likely nonetheless that San Simeon hosted at least some trade during the mission period.

For the period of the land-grant ranchos that followed Mexican independence in 1821 and the secularization and decline of the missions in the 1830s, the history of San Simeon is less elusive though still quite sketchy. In addition to Alfred Robinson, the Frenchman Eugene Duflot de Mofras, who visited San Simeon in 1841 by way of Mission San Antonio, mentioned the area in his book on California. Would that we could also cite the *Pilgrim* or the *Alert* as having called at San Simeon in the mid-1830s, but of the bay or its hinterland Richard Henry Dana, Jr., said nothing in *Two Years Before the Mast*. The *Alert* was at San Simeon in 1842, however, under Captain William Dane Phelps, who wrote in his journal of the "very snug cove well protected from the NW winds" and who also recounted a pleasant hike he took up nearby Arroyo del Puerto. Otherwise, few but the local *Californios* knew pastoral, remote San Simeon during these years before the American conquest and the eventual influx of land-hungry settlers.

In 1840 Governor Alvarado granted the prominent Jose de Jesus Pico the Rancho de la Piedra Blanca—the Ranch of the White Rock—the southernmost of Mission San Antonio's former rancho satellites. Comprising eleven leagues all told—each league in this sense encompassed nearly seven square miles—Rancho Piedra Blanca was of the maximum allowable size for a Mexican grant. Its domain extended from Arroyo del Padre Juan (the U.S. government survey later designated Pico Creek as the southern boundary), past San Simeon Bay and the white rocks that inspired the plural variant "Piedras Blancas," and on up to San Carpoforo Creek. Inland the grant encompassed the ridge that became Hearst's Enchanted Hill and continued up the main slopes of the Santa Lucias to a line just below the summit. The Hearst Ranch today includes nearly all of Rancho Piedra Blanca as it stood in the mid-nineteenth century.

Though just one league in extent, the adjoining Rancho San Simeon to the southeast, granted to Jose Ramon Estrada in 1842, was the one that took the name long identified not only with the former mission outpost but with the greater area as well—the cause, along with Cambria's having once been known as San Simeon, of no little confusion over local place names ever since. Most of this small wedge between Rancho Piedra Blanca and San Simeon Creek eventually came under Hearst ownership. So did a portion of another former rancho of Mission San Miguel, Rancho Santa Rosa, a parcel of roughly three leagues that extended from Cambria down to Harmony and that was granted in 1841 to another member of the Estrada family.

Jose de Jesus Pico and the Estrada brothers were but three among hundreds of *rancheros* in California who privately held former mission lands. Before their era was swept aside, the rancheros, according to much-romanticized tradition, led lives of aristocratic ease and plenty. They maintained huge herds of swift horses and wiry cattle, staged raucous fiestas, reared flocks of children, avoided work religiously, and rode in silver-mounted saddles over their unfenced kingdoms. The ranchos in the San Simeon area were nevertheless as isolated as the coastal holdings of Mission San Miguel and Mission San Antonio had been; on the intermittent maritime trade, therefore, the local rancheros were almost wholly dependent. Julian Estrada of Rancho Santa Rosa came the closest to realizing the arcadian ideal, as Geneva Hamilton and others have related, obtaining not only essential supplies but also luxuries and furnishings befitting his class through the coastal trade of the rancho period. Jose de Jesus Pico would undoubtedly have done the same through San Simeon Bay had he not spent most of his time away from Rancho Piedra Blanca. But enough hide-and-tallow trading was conducted in his absence to maintain a tradition that began with the missions and that extended into our own century as William Randolph Hearst brought in building materials and art works by sea.

A rare glimpse of San Simeon on the eve of California's statehood in 1850 was provided by Luman R. Slawson, an American who sailed from New York on the steamer *Sarah Sands* in December 1849, bound for San Francisco and the goldfields of the Sierra. First published in his hometown newspaper in Michigan, Slawson's letter reappeared years later in Russell E. Bidlack's article on the *Sarah Sands* in the *California Historical Society Quarterly:*

> We left [Acapulco] on the 24th [of April, 1850], and had strong head winds all the way. We got out at sea some 1500 miles and about 200 miles in longitude west of San Francisco got out of coal and had no ballast, and could not reach Montery [*sic*], about 90 miles below San Francisco, but went in a little harbor called San Simeon on the 18th of May. There is no one lives there—not a rancho within 15 miles. We lay there one day, and the captain said he would have to go back to Los Angeles, about 50 miles. But the passengers met and offered their services to fetch wood, and see if we could not get up [the coast]. We all went at it, and worked two days and got on about 40 cords of wood. Fired up at night and put out—the wind blowed harder than ever, dead ahead. We were out all night—burnt up about two-thirds of our wood; and had not made ten miles on our course—turned about and went back and anchored where we left the night before. As we went in in the morning we saw two Mexicans coming down the mountain on horse back, driving two horses. They came down to the beach and the captain went on shore and bought their horses and sent an express to San Francisco for coal. Before night those Mexicans brought down over 100 horses and sold a good many for $100 apiece. Over 150 of the passengers left and went by

land from here, rather than wait for coal, but we stuck to the "old Sally" yet and as it turned out we did well, for those that went across had a hard time. We enjoyed ourselves well, and had sport seeing the Mexicans lasso the beef. The captain made a bargain with them to furnish him with two beeves every day we staid there. They would drive them right down on the beach and lasso them wherever the butcher told them to. They were the fattest and best beef I ever saw, and no wonder, for there is over 20,000 acres of wild oats here, some in the ravines higher than I could reach. We all took our tents ashore and had a time, to see how it would seem when we got to the diggins. Our coal came and we left for good on the 3d of June, after laying here most three weeks, and landed safe and sound at San Francisco the 5th. They all thought we were lost, as they had not heard anything of us since we left Acapulco, but "old Sally" carried us safe.

The Mexicans mentioned in Slawson's letter were most likely some of Jose de Jesus Pico's *vaqueros* on Rancho Piedra Blanca.

For all their seeming wealth in land and livestock, Pico and his kind were ill-equipped to survive the 1850s and '60s. The Land Act of 1851 put the burden of proof upon them as they sought to have their land titles recognized by a new authority,

When the steamer Sarah Sands *ran out of coal on its passage from New York to San Francisco in 1850, it laid over in San Simeon Bay until help arrived more than two weeks later. "There is no one lives there—not a rancho within 15 miles," wrote Luman R. Slawson, one of the passengers. Actually, there were three ranchos within that distance, but the remoteness and solitude of the area in 1850 must have made them seem nonexistent. The captain arranged for two* vaqueros, *probably from Rancho Piedra Blanca, to drive two beeves to the beach every day to feed the passengers and crew. Slawson described the cattle as "the fattest and best beef" he had ever seen.*

the United States. Litigation could drag on for years, leaving many a Californio the victim of legal fees and usurious interest rates before his grant was confirmed and patented; in the meantime squatterism gnawed away at the ranchos. Relations between Californios and "Yankees" increasingly deteriorated until the old guard was nearly as maligned as California's Chinese population. Providence itself dealt a stinging and often final blow in the great drought of 1862-64, which decimated livestock and parched the land. Pico of Piedra Blanca was ruined, as were many of his fellow Californios. His rancho, though finally patented in his name in 1876, changed hands completely by the end of the 1870s, mostly through a series of sales to George Hearst, a rich mining baron and the father of Wiliam Randolph Hearst.

San Simeon was already emerging from the sleepy isolation of the rancho period when George Hearst arrived in 1865—two years after his son had been born in San Francisco—and bought some 30,000 acres of Piedra Blanca, the first of many parcels he bought from Jose de Jesus Pico and others in the greater area. More than 17,000 acres of Piedra Blanca had been sold as early as 1854; and before Hearst's arrival other newcomers had gained a foothold in the district, mostly by settling on public-domain lands or by squatting on the remaining grant acreage. This modest population boom prompted an increase in shipping activity at San Simeon Bay. Dairying, agriculture, and ranching were beginning to replace the antiquated Mexican cattle industry the drought had destroyed; each depended on San Simeon Bay for connections with distant markets. The most colorful new venture was the shore-whaling station the Portuguese Joseph Clark had established on San Simeon Point in 1864, one of several such operations eventually strung along the entire length of the California coast. For the next thirty years Captain Clark and his crews pursued a majestic quarry, the California gray whales that annually migrate from the Gulf of Alaska to Baja California and back again, passing close to

San Simeon each way. Twenty-two whales made up an average year's catch during Clark's first decade at San Simeon, a respectable showing for a shore-based operation.

Mining was also becoming important in the nearby Santa Lucias. Like the other new enterprises, it depended on coastal shipping though San Simeon Bay. Cinnabar, much sought after at the time for the mercury it yielded, was discovered in the early 1860s; by 1871 the Pine Mountain Mining District had been formed. Four years later the lure of gold in the wilds south of Big Sur brought the Los Burros Mining District into being, its southern boundary marked by San Carpoforo Creek—"Sankypoky," as some of the crusty miners called it. George Hearst had gone through a crusty period himself, first in the lead mines of his native Missouri and then in the goldfields of California. But the fabulous Comstock Lode stood between Hearst's rough-and-ready days and his new role as the Baron of San Simeon. Evidently he was content to let the local mining rushes run their course while he concentrated on developing his portion of Piedra Blanca.

The 1870s marked the emergence of the actual town of San Simeon about half a mile leeward of Joseph Clark's whaling station; the 1870s also saw George Hearst expand his own interests in the area mightily. Next to the town, he built a new wharf, the big freight shed of which still stands near Sebastians's Store, a fellow survivor of the era along with the one-room Pacific School and the lighthouse on Point Piedras Blancas. A short distance inland he built a handsome two-story Italianate ranch house that remains in use. He continued to add Piedra Blanca and other acreage to his vast holdings. (After Hearst acquired part of Rancho Santa Rosa, Francisco "Don Pancho" Estrada, son of the original grantee, became *mayordomo* of Piedra Blanca, a position he still held honorarily in his graybeard days under William Randolph Hearst.) And as especially suited a Californian of his stature, George Hearst stocked his ranch with prize thoroughbreds, a venture that

Mrs. William Randolph Hearst, Jr., has richly portrayed in *The Horses of San Simeon.*

In addition to Mrs. Hearst's book, Mrs. Fremont Older's invaluable *William Randolph Hearst: American* contains many details of local history, among them a recounting of the conditions that prevailed before George Hearst improved his Piedra Blanca property. For example, George's wife, Phoebe Apperson Hearst, did not visit the ranch until the new wharf was built in 1878, according to Mrs. Older, for "the journey was rough even for men. Sometimes father and son went on a coast steamer. At San Simeon Bay they were met by a small tug. The transfer from the steamer to the small boat was hair-raising, but the excitement of landing in the tug delighted Will." (The last sentence refers to the lighters that had to be used before 1878 for passengers and freight.) Mrs. Older also related that George Hearst and his son sometimes went from San Francisco to Paso Robles by train, although she must have meant by stagecoach, since no rails reached that far south until 1886. At any rate, upon arriving at Paso Robles, the Hearsts were "met by vaqueros with saddled horses. Then back they rode over the mountains by way of Cayucos"—on the Old Creek trail—"and up the coast to the ranch-house." She further recounted the younger Hearst's riding to San Simeon through the Big Sur country. "At times Will Hearst and his friends chose the wildest route to San Simeon along the coast over the

Until Rancho Piedra Blanca was patented in Jose de Jesus Pico's name in 1876, George Hearst and others who had bought portions of the ranch had no clear title to their holdings. By 1878 George Hearst was free to develop his thousands of Piedra Blanca acres without further encumbrance. In addition to improving the wharfage at San Simeon Bay, Hearst built a two-story house a short distance inland along Arroyo del Puerto, where the stately old home remains today, hidden among tall eucalyptus and other trees.

mountains from Monterey," she wrote. "They camped by night looking out on the Pacific. On one of these journeys their supply of butter gave out and Will rode into the camp of a man named Pringle who had a gold mine on the coast. He asked for butter. Pringle stared at him and replied, 'Butter! What in hell is that? I haven't seen any in twenty years.'"

Once San Simeon became more accessible, Phoebe Hearst made her first trips to Piedra Blanca. She had learned to ride while growing up in Missouri, "and often she and her friends went on camping trips into the mountains," Mrs. Older wrote in her biography of William Randolph Hearst. "They frequently stopped on what today is known as *La Cuesta Encantada,* or 'The Enchanted Hill.' George Hearst especially liked the thicket of oaks on the crest of the elevation, and he never tired of looking at the sea from this point. The camping place was called Camp Hill." Elsewhere in the same book she related, "To this remote, romantic ranch Senator Hearst brought his son and his friends for fishing, hunting and camping. On the crest of what is now called the Enchanted Hill, the Senator erected a cabin, and the elevation was known as Camp Hill." (The elder Hearst, it should be noted, was not actually a senator until 1886.) Winifred Black Bonfils, the original sob sister "Annie Laurie" of the Hearst press, also referred to the camp in her *Life and Personality of Phoebe Apperson Hearst*: "High in the Santa Lucia mountains that mark the California coastline with wild and rugged beauty, there was an old camp ground where William Randolph Hearst had often gone on a fishing expedition with his father, the Senator." In the early 1930s William Randolph Hearst himself described old Camp Hill to the bookman A. Edward Newton, who recounted his visit to San Simeon in *The Atlantic Monthly.* "It was a favorite spot of my father's," Hearst told Newton, "and I love it. I used to come up here with him as a boy. In those days we had a little cabin just about where we are now sitting." In the absence of primary source material, brief passages like these are the best references that exist on the Camp Hill of the 1870s and '80s.

Now that the era of western excursioning had dawned, the Hearsts could regard Piedra Blanca as their exclusive answer to the hot springs, the natural wonderlands, the grand resorts the rich were frequenting, a place where they could enjoy a life of comfortable rusticity. Memories and traditions naturally grew out of the halcyon days of Camp Hill. William Randolph Hearst later quipped that he had ascended the 1,600-foot slope by hanging on to the tail of his pony.

When George Hearst became a United States Senator in 1886, he and Phoebe Hearst moved from San Francisco to Washington, D.C. Their son began his legendary publishing career in 1887 with the *San Francisco Examiner.* With George's death in 1891, Phoebe's increasing devotion to philanthropy and travel, and William Randolph's move to New York in 1895 to assume ownership of his second newspaper, the *New York Morning Journal,* San Simeon, Piedra Blanca, and Camp Hill faded into the background. Phoebe Hearst eventually returned to California and her country estate near Pleasanton, the Hacienda del Pozo de Verona; her trips to Piedra Blanca became infrequent, though she did add to her late husband's land holdings in the area. Even her son appears to have visited the ranch infrequently—business, politics, and, after 1903, a family of his own kept him in the east most of the time. What trips he did make to California revolved around his newspapers in San Francisco and Los Angeles and his mother's Pleasanton home. San Simeon meanwhile lapsed into quiet isolation after the Southern Pacific reached San Luis Obispo in 1894, especially after "the gap" remaining between there and Santa Barbara was finally closed in 1901. The use of San Simeon Bay fell off sharply, and the bustling days of the later 1800s became a distant memory. Soon after his horseback trip through the area in 1911, J. Smeaton Chase wrote of San Simeon in *California Coast Trails,* "This once promising little port has dwindled under the caprices of Fortune and local landowners until now only one small coasting steamer calls unpunctually at its wharf. I found myself the only guest in a hotel that would have housed double the whole population, with room to spare." After 1915 coastal steamers ceased to call even unpunctually for passengers or freight.

After the Great War broke out in Europe, William Randolph Hearst, who was entering his fifties, began making longer and more frequent trips to California. It was then, as William Randolph Hearst, Jr., later recalled, that Hearst took his young family down to San Simeon for one of the first times after a customary stopover at Grandmother Hearst's. Perhaps by then the thought of building on the ranch was beginning to turn in his mind; perhaps, in fact, it had already been turning for several years. Mrs. Fremont Older indicated that at least once during his congressional career (1903-1907), Hearst had vacationed on the ranch and that he had ridden over the hills and had "planned to erect a house on the summit of one where he had camped as a boy." She also related that after his dramatic bid for the governorship of New York in 1906, Hearst had written to his mother of his love for California, concluding with *"Vive le ranch!* I am going to save up and build a cabin down at the ranch just big enough for you and Millie and the baby and me." (The baby was named George for his grandfather and was the first of five sons born to Hearst and

The late J.C. "Pete" Sebastian was a window into a bygone era of Mexican miners, Portuguese whalers, Swiss dairymen, and Japanese abalone divers—and into a nearly as bygone era of Hollywood stars and world celebrities. The store that Pete's father bought in 1914, and that Pete himself later owned, consisted of two smaller store buildings that were combined in 1878; one of the two had originally been built on San Simeon Point near Joseph Clark's whaling station. Sebastian's Store remains in business today, its display of Captain Clark's whaling gear making it a museum of local history.

his wife, Millicent, from 1904 to 1915; George was followed by William, Jr., John, and twins Randolph and David.) Until 1919 Hearst may indeed have hoped to build something "just big enough" at San Simeon; his cabin of 1906 recalls his father's cabin of the early years and is also similar to his bungalow of 1919. But it would seem unlike Hearst not to have had a greater hope—or rather a dream—for San Simeon after that long. At any rate, the memorable summer days of old Camp Hill were revived during the war, but now with tents on portable wood floors where once George Hearst's cabin had stood.

Phoebe Hearst was now in her seventies and "could never be induced to take part in the rough camp life," according to Winifred Black Bonfils, "but she had frequent letters from the campers and she used to say that she enjoyed camping out 'vicariously' very much indeed. One letter in particular gave her some idea of the joys of life at San Simeon and she treasured it carefully all the rest of her life." That letter, from Hearst to his mother, probably dates from the summer of 1917 or 1918:

> If you could see your son and your grandsons today on the ranch you would be highly entertained and pleased too.
>
> William is a regular husky. He has gotten tanned and strong and he eats like a hired man. Everybody wonders where he puts it all and there are various suggestions such as a hollow leg and a patent expansion stomach. None seems quite sufficient to explain the remarkable disappearance of grub into the child.
>
> John is well and fresh and finds it hard work to explain some of the lies he told the rest of the children about his remarkable exploits on the ranch when here before. . . .
>
> We have been up to the Sancho Pojo [San Carpoforo] and rode from there up the coast for ten or twelve miles. We went last night up to Pat Garrity's [an old homestead below Garrity Peak] and camped. This morning the two youngest woke us all up at half past *four*.
>
> We had breakfast and then came down to the Arroyo La

Cruz and went in swimming in a big pool, first the children, then the girls and finally the men.

When Guy [Barham] & I came out we sent George on horseback over to the little temporary camp for a towel. He came back in a minute with it &—lazy as usual—tried to hand us the towel without getting off his horse. He rode the horse to the edge of the pool & the first thing George knew the horse went right into the pool and swam across. In the middle of the pool George slid off and swam ashore. He was sopping of course. So he took off his clothes and dried them on a hot rock and this gave him an excuse for going in swimming again.

We are back in our regular camp at the top of the hill now tired and *sleepy* on account of those kids. I love this ranch. It is wonderful. I love the sea and I love the mountains and the hollows in the hills and the shady places in the creeks and the fine old oaks and even the hot brushy hillsides—full of quail—and the canyons full of deer. It's a wonderful place. I would rather spend a month here than any place in the world. And as a sanitarium!! Mother it has Nauheim, Carlsbad, Vichy, Wiesbaden, French Lick, Saratoga and every other so-called health resort beaten a nautical mile.

Little did Hearst realize he would soon be pursuing a dream that seems unmistakable in those words, a dream far greater than anything he had previously conceived. Phoebe Apperson Hearst died in 1919, a victim of the influenza epidemic that swept the country after the war. Her son inherited Rancho Piedra Blanca and other choice properties. Poised on the brink of the expansive 1920s, William Randolph Hearst now had the wherewithal to move mountains—almost literally.

"I Had No Idea When We Began to Build . . ."

WITH A GREAT family fortune now his, William Randolph Hearst was ideally equipped to begin building at San Simeon. Although his project began modestly in 1919, it quickly assumed greater proportions; by the mid-1920s it assumed regal proportions. Hearst's wealth, vision, and enthusiasm carried him far into the 1930s as well, despite the Depression. Even the Second World War proved but a temporary obstacle: Hearst resumed building in 1945 at the age of eighty-two. Only the insurmountable forces of old age and failing health were enough to bring Hearst's pursuit of his dream to a permanent halt in the late 1940s.

To return to 1919 and to Hearst in his mid-fifties, we find a man who, shortly before his mother died on April 13, had been thinking about improving Camp Hill. The recollections of Walter Steilberg, a longtime friend and former employee of Hearst's architect, Julia Morgan, are especially illuminating in this regard. Steilberg recalled that in 1919—apparently a week or two before Phoebe Hearst's death—Hearst had dropped by Morgan's office in the Merchants Exchange Building in San

Francisco. Steilberg paraphrased Hearst's having told Morgan, "I would like to build something up on the hill at San Simeon. I get tired of going up there and camping in tents. I'm getting a little old for that. I'd like to get something that would be more comfortable."

Hearst had a book with him, a "bungalow book" that contained a "Jappo-Swisso" example. Steilberg recalled that Hearst and Morgan had chuckled at the term and that Hearst had said it was the simplicity of the example, not the style, that he found appealing.*

Hearst seemingly was still visualizing something modest, perhaps even something nearly as modest as the cabin he had mentioned in 1906—at least until his mother died and the prospect of a great inheritance materialized. But wasn't Hearst a veteran newspaperman who normally took quick, decisive action in his quest for spectacular results? Hadn't he shown a propensity toward building in the grand manner from as early as the 1890s? And hadn't the Camp Hill of the last few summers been ambitious in its own right? His apparent modesty—however we might explain it—is ultimately of little importance; for, as Walter Steilberg recalled, Hearst was not long in showing his true colors; soon after his mother's death, he began to think much more ambitiously about San Simeon.

Mrs. Fremont Older's equivalent of the "bungalow" episode in her authorized biography of Hearst is not to be overlooked. Mrs. Older indicated—somewhat between the lines, as she often did—that after the summer of 1918 Hearst wanted to avoid the dismantling of Camp Hill in the future. "During the winter there was much destruction from the elements or

---

*The recollections of Walter Steilberg cited in this book are from interviews conducted by Sally Woodbridge in 1974 as part of the Julia Morgan Architectural History Project, Regional Oral History Office, The Bancroft Library, University of California, Berkeley. In 1966 Steilberg addressed a group of employees from Hearst San Simeon State Historical Monument; his paraphrase of the conversation between Hearst and Morgan in 1919 was essentially the same as in 1974, although he referred to a "Swisso-Jappo" rather than a "Jappo-Swisso" bungalow.

rodents," she wrote. "Labor and repairing were necessary to put the Camp in order for summer. In 1919"—sometime before Phoebe Hearst's death—"Hearst said to Miss Julia Morgan, the architect, that he would like to have plans drawn for a permanent camp of spacious, cool, comfortable concrete build-ings with tiled floors, where he could place his large collection of Indian rugs. He wished to avoid the annual seasonal set-ups and repairs entailed by portable tent houses." But after his mother died, Hearst "decided to create a new home on Camp Hill. The plans for the permanent summer camp were en-larged. Hearst now desired a residence with spacious living quarters, having the informality and hospitality of the summer camp." Whichever version we take as a premise, Steilberg's or Mrs. Older's, Hearst clearly was ready to plunge into the new venture with his characteristic zeal well before the year 1919 was out. (Years later an old friend of the Hearst family recalled having been at Camp Hill in 1917 when Hearst unveiled a model of his proposed "castle"; no such unveiling seems pos-sible, though, before 1919.)

Julia Morgan was as ready as Hearst was. Easily the most accomplished woman in the history of American architec-ture—and for that matter one of this country's most accom-plished architects regardless of gender—Morgan was ap-proaching the mid-point in a career that would span the first half of the twentieth century, during which she would design hundreds of buildings besides those for William Randolph Hearst, her commissions ranging up and down California and occasionally farther afield. Known both as a versatile problem-solver and as a sympathetic "client's architect," Julia Morgan was a wise choice on Hearst's part, as the complexities and demands of the San Simeon job continually proved.

Hearst's choice was not only wise but predictable as well. Around 1912 he and Julia Morgan planned a residence for his property in Sausalito, a project that never materialized beyond the building of a hillside retaining wall. Shortly thereafter they built a cabin on Hearst's Grandview Point property at the South Rim of the Grand Canyon. During this same period their Los Angeles Examiner Building was impressively conceived and carried out, a prelude to the grandeur of San Simeon. Even as early as 1903, after Julia Morgan returned from the Beaux-Arts in Paris and began working on Phoebe Hearst's Hacienda del Pozo de Verona near Pleasanton, their paths crossed, on this occasion apparently for the first time. Hearst "supervised alterations in the Hacienda," according to Mrs. Fremont Older's biography, "consulting with the young architect, Julia Morgan, a small unassuming genius. . . . This meeting was the foundation of a significant connection in Hearst's life."

William Randolph Hearst was undoubtedly one of the greatest romantics who ever lived. Julia Morgan, in her own modest way, was highly idealistic and romantic too. With one arm she embraced the modernism that was coming of age; with the other she clung to a past that was too sustaining to relinquish. In Hearst she had a client—a patron, he might better be called—who mirrored her deep-seated interest in the Middle Ages and the Renaissance. San Simeon and other Hearst commissions enabled Morgan to pursue that interest to the utmost.

How did William Randolph Hearst and Julia Morgan decide on the work to be done at San Simeon? Did Hearst take the

The Camp Hill of George Hearst's day apparently consisted of a cabin, though no such structure seems to have existed when William Randolph Hearst resumed the use of Camp Hill during World War I. The son's latter-day camp consisted of a tent village—a main social and dining tent accompanied by outlying sleeping and service tents. By the early part of 1919 Hearst was making plans to replace Camp Hill with a "bungalow" or a "permanent camp," the descriptions differing in the two leading accounts; but after his mother's death in April his plans quickly assumed a grander scale.

lead, or did he have to rely on Morgan? Questions like these have been asked repeatedly for years. Mrs. Fremont Older quoted Julia Morgan as saying that Hearst and she were "fellow architects," that Hearst loved "architecting," that he would have been "a great architect" had he chosen that career—an important, revealing passage, but one that was too brief by itself to provide lasting answers. What was needed was firsthand documentary insight into Hearst and Morgan's working relationship, yet the prospect that such documentation would materialize seemed remote. Many believed, for instance, that Julia Morgan burned her papers upon retirement—her final act in her long commitment to anonymity. This disheartening belief, however, stemmed mainly from too literal an interpretation of Morgan's philosophy that her buildings should "speak for themselves."

What actually happened was that after more than forty years of practice Julia Morgan needed to clean house in her Merchants Exchange office. Her business records, correspondence, photographs, drawings, and other papers went in at least two directions. One portion was retained by H.C. Forney, who had worked as Hearst's valuation engineer through Julia Morgan's office and whose wife had been Morgan's secretary for many years. (Mrs. Forney maintains that, aside from some blueprints, none of Morgan's papers were destroyed; in recent years her daughter has given numerous Morgan drawings from the family's holdings to the University of California, Berkeley.) Another portion—a portion that Morgan herself retained—subsequently passed into the hands of her nephew, Morgan North. Most of this portion was given to California Polytechnic State Universtiy, San Luis Obispo, in 1980 by Mrs. Morgan North and is the core of that institution's Julia Morgan Collection. Mrs. North's gift included extensive correspondence between Hearst and Morgan concerning San Simeon. These documents and other items in the collection have conclusively answered many long-standing questions. In fact, the

Julia Morgan Collection—though it is but a portion of the surviving whole—is rich enough by itself to have revolutionized almost overnight our knowledge of William Randolph Hearst, Julia Morgan, San Simeon, and numerous related subjects.

(The situation recalls that of another figure of the period, President Warren G. Harding. Forty years after Harding's death a collection of papers materialized, a collection many believed had been burned, providing a far more balanced view of the man and his times. As was once aptly said of the need for archival sources, "No documents, no history.")

The San Simeon correspondence corroborates Morgan's statement that she and Hearst were "fellow architects"; it likewise corroborates Walter Steilberg's having said of them that he wouldn't have been surprised "to see a spark traveling from one skull to the other, back and forth, because those two very different people just clicked." For all their uncommon rapport, however, center stage unquestionably belonged to William Randolph Hearst, as well it should have, since his grandiose dream, his aspirations, his whimsical flights of fancy, his dynastic wealth fired the epic project at every turn. For the protagonist Hearst, Julia Morgan played the finest supporting role of her career. Their relationship was thoroughly congenial, corroborative, and, at the same time, professional. To the very end of their long collaboration they addressed each other in a somewhat old-fashioned but always dignified way as "Mr. Hearst" and "Miss Morgan."

Hearst had lived in New York since 1895, and he continued to live there until the mid-1920s. With three thousand miles separating him from Julia Morgan in San Francisco—a far greater distance in 1919 than today—consultation by letter and telegram was imperative if Hearst was to stay as involved as possible in the new project. Hearst's business correspondence was already indispensable in his masterminding of his publishing empire; Julia Morgan now became, in effect, another of

Hearst's top lieutenants with whom he regularly communicated. From the very outset, therefore, the Hearst-Morgan correspondence played a critical, decisive part in the planning and execution of the work at San Simeon.

The earliest surviving correspondence dates from August 1919, when the Hearsts were in residence at Camp Hill, and draws the curtains back on events already in progress. By then a few months had passed since Hearst and Morgan first discussed a "bungalow" and a "permanent camp"; a considerably bolder idea had emerged, an idea of an "architectural group" of buildings reminiscent of a European hill town, in which a towered structure would dominate the setting. Hearst had come a long way since his original proposals, but his dream was still somewhat embryonic. Surely he was thinking of much smaller and simpler structures than we see today when he told Julia Morgan that he wanted the main central unit built first and ready for use by the summer of 1920 and that the outlying units in the group could be ready by the summer of 1921. How Mr. Hearst and Miss Morgan must have smiled if ever in later years they paused to recall that first summer!

As soon as Hearst returned to New York in the fall of 1919, he took up the question of the smaller, outlying buildings. The site had to be determined for the trio that became known simply as "the houses," as did a great many other details such

From her Merchants Exchange office in San Francisco, Julia Morgan ran one of California's leading architectural firms for more than forty years. Renowned for her high standards and for her attention to the minutest details, Miss Morgan was steadily in demand in her chosen field. William Randolph Hearst was just one of her many clients, though he was certainly one of her most important over the years—and certainly her most colorful and dynamic. San Simeon posed endless challenges and complications, but that commission was perhaps the most fulfilling one of all for her.

as their size, scale, and floor plan as well as the materials to be used in their construction and decoration. Far removed from the subject of his emerging dream, Hearst depended on his correspondence with Julia Morgan to keep him in close touch. In a letter dated October 25, 1919, he encouraged her to take good advantage of the natural beauty of the region, stating that the view was the "main thing at the ranch." In the same letter he informed her he had decided to hold off on starting the main building until the houses were completed, which he hoped would be in time for his summer vacation in 1920.*

The grandeur that even the houses would eventually embody and the important role they would play in the overall architectural scheme became more apparent as Hearst and Morgan compared notes. Before the first year was out, Hearst could write, "We refer to them as little houses, but they are not really little houses. They are only little as compared to the big central building." As to their site, Hearst emphasized that they shouldn't be built too far down the side of the hill lest the main building seem "ashamed of them." "They could be treated that way if they were servants' quarters or out-buildings of small importance," Hearst said, "but as they are dwelling houses of consequence, and very pretty buildings, I think they should be brought more into the general composition, and treated as attractive features of it." He concluded by saying that landscape design would eventually unify all the buildings, producing a "harmonious whole," a conception magnificently realized in the years ahead. Hearst's powers of visualization were clearly in evidence now.

Hearst and Morgan also weighed the question of architectural style, making some important choices that, to a greater or lesser degree, influenced most of the work at San Simeon for more than two decades. At least as early as September 1919 they

---

* The Hearst-Morgan and related correspondence cited in this book is from the Julia Morgan Collection, Special Collections and University Archives, Robert E. Kennedy Library, California Polytechnic State University, San Luis Obispo.

considered the Cathedral of Santa Maria la Mayor in Ronda, Spain, as an inspiration for the towers of the main building. By then they had apparently decided that the historical character of their architectural group should be Spanish—the choice was appropriate, romantically speaking, in view of San Simeon's early heritage—but they still had to decide upon the particular type or period of Spanish architecture. They consulted some of the recent books on the subject, among them Arthur Byne and Mildred Stapley's *Spanish Architecture of the Sixteenth Century* and especially Austin Whittlesey's *Minor Ecclesiastical, Domestic and Garden Architecture of Southern Spain.* Several motifs for the buildings were ultimately derived from these two books. In a letter dictated in New York on the last day of 1919, Hearst discussed the question in detail:

> I have thought a great deal over whether to make this whole group of buildings Baroc, in the Eighteenth Century style, or Renaissance.
>
> It is quite a problem. I started out with the Baroc idea in mind, as nearly all the Spanish architecture in America is of that character. . . .
>
> If we should decide on this style, I would at least want to depart from the very crude and rude examples of it that we have in our early California Spanish architecture.
>
> The Mission at Santa Barbara is doubtless the highest example of this California architecture, and yet it is very bare and almost clumsy to my mind.
>
> The best things I have seen in this Spanish Baroc are at the San Diego Exposition. . . .
>
> I understand that the San Diego Exposition stuff is largely reproductions from the best examples in Mexico and South America, and that we could not go to a better source to get the most agreeable specimens of this style.
>
> This style at its best is sufficiently satisfactory, though in our early California architecture it seems to me too primitive, and in many examples I have seen in Mexico so elaborate as to be objectionable.

Between these two extremes, however, there are good examples and I think the San Diego Exposition affords the best. . . .

The alternative is to build this group of buildings in the Renaissance style of Southern Spain. We picked out the towers of the Church of Ronda. I suppose they are Renaissance or else transitional, and they have some Gothic feeling; but a Renaissance decoration, particularly that of the very southern part of Spain, would harmonize well with them.

The Renaissance of Northern Spain seems to me very hard, while the Renaissance of Southern Spain is much softer and more graceful.

We get very beautiful decoration both for the central building and for the cottages [the houses] out of this Southern Spain Renaissance style, and I think that would, in the main, be the best period for interior decoration.

The trouble would be, I suppose, that it has no historic association with California, or rather with the Spanish architecture in California. . . .

. . . But after all, would it not be better to do something a little different than other people are doing out in California as long as we do not do anything incongruous?

Therefore, as you see, I am inclined to a pretty harmonious Renaissance treatment all through for the main building and the cottages as well.

Julia Morgan's response of January 8, 1920, showed how productive their correspondence could be and how, in the best interests of the project, she felt at liberty to disagree, something Hearst often encouraged her to do:

Two years ago work took me down to San Diego very frequently and I know the buildings well. The composition and decoration are certainly very well handled indeed, but I question whether this type of decoration would not seem too heavy and clumsy on our buildings, because while the Exposition covers acres with its buildings, we have a comparatively small group, and it would seem to me that they should charm by their detail rather than overwhelm by more or less clumsy exuberance.

I feel just as you do about the early California Mission style as being too primitive to be gone back to and copied. . . . As I wrote you in my last letter, I believe we could get something really very beautiful [for the main building] by using a combination of Ronda Towers and the Sevilla doorway [in Austin Whittlesey's book].

On January 14 Hearst telegrammed Morgan, "Our definite decision in favor of the Renaissance makes it unnecessary to go into the San Diego Exposition stuff at all." The plural "Our" in this context seemingly alludes to Hearst and his wife, who shared her husband's enthusiasm for San Simeon in the early years. (It was Millicent Hearst, for instance, who began calling the hilltop Las Estrellas in 1921, a name used until the more dramatic La Cuesta Encantada was chosen in 1924.) More likely, however, the plural form alludes to a decision jointly made by Hearst, with whom Mrs. Hearst concurred, and Morgan—an instance of their acting as "fellow architects." In any event, Southern Spanish Renaissance was the choice. From that premise William Randolph Hearst and Julia Morgan eventually created for San Simeon a style distinctly Mediterranean in spirit but a style that has never lent itself to more exact nomenclature. Attempts at codification have ranged from the coy to the serious—from Early Hollywood to Spanish Colonial Revival—yet none of them has quite hit the mark. Perhaps the style should simply be called Hearstian, a style—and a nonstyle—uniquely its own. In that uniqueness lies part of the charm and beauty, the magic and romance of San Simeon.

The selection of an architectural style was not the only challenge to be met that first winter. On the local front, Julia Morgan, who also had to act as general contractor, had her hands full with more prosaic matters, among them the quagmires that rural California roads became each year once the rains set in. Conditions were scarcely less primitive in 1920 than they had been decades earlier for the Californios, whose lumbering oxcarts were no match for the ubiquitous mud. Trucks were in use by 1920, but the hauling of materials from the railhead in San Luis Obispo was laborious at best; the trip to the hilltop building site from the town of San Simeon, where Hearst had set up warehousing in the old freight shed of 1878, could be especially grueling. Horses and mules were used when the trucks faltered. Rugged conditions also prevailed in the winter of 1921; Julia Morgan reported on February 4 that year that she had reached "the Top" during her last trip to San Simeon "with the aid of a four mule road team part way." "The county road by the Los Osos Valley above the lagoon is in inexcusable shape," she explained in the same letter, "and elsewhere the ruts are so deep the low type autos simply cannot make it." And a year later still, Morgan wrote, "If you would like to break every bone in your worst enemy's body treat him to the trip from Cayucos to Cambria."

Early shipments by sea from San Francisco to San Simeon Bay posed just as much of a challenge. The weather, once again, could be a great obstacle; so could the condition of the ships themselves. In November 1919 Julia Morgan reported the

"Voilà! You've captured it perfectly, Miss Morgan. That's just what I had in mind." Though no such words are recorded anywhere, we can easily imagine Hearst's having said something like them on many occasions. He and Julia Morgan not only corresponded regularly about San Simeon, especially through the 1920s, but also spent much time on the job site poring over drawings and plans. Hearst himself roughed out a sketch at times, leaving the finer points to Morgan, who in turn left final approval to him. Their sense of give and take was remarkable for any client and architect, for this or for any other era. The two were truly the "fellow architects" Morgan once said they were.

46

sailing of the *Cleone,* "a very disreputable old coaster," which nevertheless made port at San Simeon without incident. Not so the *Admiral Nicholson,* which sprang a leak as it entered San Simeon Bay in April 1920; the load of plaster and cement stored below decks was damaged. Two weeks later Morgan wrote, "Bad weather outside has put the shipping schedules out again. The 'Nicholson' could not even put in at Monterey Bay this trip and had to bring her cargo back." A year later Morgan wrote that the same ship had "sprung a more serious leak than usual" and that the construction crew had "had no transportation for a month."

Morgan also had trouble assembling an adequate work force, despite Hearst's authorizing her to pay premium wages as an inducement. Unsettled postwar conditions, especially in a tightly unionized city like San Francisco, were mostly to blame; the new decade had dawned, but the twenties boom—the "Coolidge prosperity"—was still far in the future. When the problems Julia Morgan faced that first winter are considered, it is remarkable that construction actually began on the three houses in February 1920, several weeks before the rainy season was slated to end. It soon became apparent, however, that it would be impossible to complete them in time for the Hearst's summer visit. In April the situation remained largely the same, as Morgan reported to Hearst in New York:

> The shortages of every kind of material and of workmen out here is incredible, from draughtsmen to window glass inclusive.... I had to take one of the modelers up to San Simeon this week and convince him that it was a "lovely place" and then have him telephone from there back to the shop that I was veracious, before the cast-cement crew would agree to go up....
>
> You were evidently right about getting a country trained builder, for I do not believe we could have held a city man. The San Francisco men sent down on the "bonus" plan have nearly all come back, one turned back at San Simeon, some

got to the top of the hill and did not unpack, and some stayed a week or more. They all agreed that the living conditions, money and food were all right, but they "didn't like feeling so far away from things." Mr. Washburn is picking up "country" men as fast as he can.

One of superintendent Herbert Washburn's new country men was Frank Souza of Cambria, who became labor foreman and stayed on for many years. Other locals also hired on. One of them was more a country *boy* in 1920, fourteen-year-old J.C. "Pete" Sebastian of San Simeon, who recalled that he rode his horse up to Hearst Camp each Monday morning that summer, stayed on the hill to work the rest of the week, and rode back down late Saturday for his day off. The employment of local help was a boon to the new project, but there would always be a need for highly skilled city men; San Simeon's fine wood carving, wrought iron work, plaster and cast stone decoration, tile work, and other contemporary efforts are sure indications that Hearst and Morgan succeeded in recruiting the necessary talent. Theodore Van der Loo was the first master craftsman to work at San Simeon, coming down from Oakland in 1920 to get the cast stone decoration under way for the three houses; more than twenty years later his son John was still doing work for the main building. Later in 1920 Frank Humrich and his crew came out from New York, apparently having been recruited there by Hearst; among them was a Hungarian named Frank Gyorgy who stayed on into the 1930s and whose versatility as an architectural decorator proved indispensable. Other master craftsmen were soon commissioned to produce decorative items in their Los Angeles or Bay Area workshops for installation at San Simeon. Jules Suppo of San Francisco, for example, was kept busy for several years carving ornamental woodwork. Fellow San Franciscans F. M. Lorenz, an equally skilled woodcarver, and L. Cardini, a marble sculptor, also turned out large quantities of work for San Simeon in their studios. Ed Trinkkeller of Los Angeles produced a variety of decorative ironwork in his studio near the Examiner Building, which he had worked on earlier for Hearst and Morgan. Still other names can be mentioned; but many cannot, having been lost in the maze of historical details surrounding San Simeon. The various workers, from the day laborers on Frank Souza's concrete crew to the masters of Jules Suppo's stature, played vital roles in Hearst's pursuit of his dream. They have rightly been called the unsung heroes of the hill.

Despite mud, rain, leaky ships, waterfront strikes, shortages of materials, homesick craftsmen, and other problems, Julia Morgan made significant headway that first winter. True, there was no prospect of completing the houses as soon as Hearst had hoped; but the progress to date was remarkable, and Hearst was well aware of it. Orrin Peck, Hearst's lifelong friend and an accomplished painter who helped plan some of the early decorative schemes for San Simeon, let Julia Morgan know that her work had not gone unnoticed. From New York, where he was staying with the Hearsts in the spring of 1920, Peck wrote to Morgan, "Expect you have had a devil of a time getting the houses as far along as they are—Will appreciates your efforts—& difficulties surmounted & realizes it was no picnic."

The Hearsts returned in the summer of 1920 for what proved to be their last season in their hilltop tents. In the summer of 1921 the family was able for the first time to make somewhat improvised use of the houses, which still remained

The three houses were richly decorated with plasterwork based mostly on Spanish motifs, many of which Hearst and Morgan derived from photographs. In contrast, several doors and doorways in Casa del Sol's lower suite were copied from antique architectural elements Hearst bought through the art market in the early 1920s. A Hungarian craftsman named Frank Gyorgy was in charge of painting and gilding the plaster reproductions; his signature, dated 1924, has been found atop the cornice on the left.

unfinished. Nineteen twenty-two was an off year; after returning from Europe in June, Hearst was unable to break away
from commitments in the east long enough to visit the ranch.
This gave Julia Morgan until 1923 to continue working on the
houses. Even then a number of loose ends remained, but the
Hearsts' tents could now be dispensed with for good.

By 1923 the focal point had shifted to what was eventually
named Casa Grande, the huge main building that Morgan's
new superintendent, Camille Rossi, had started the previous
summer and that now loomed over the houses as a rough
concrete hulk. By the end of 1923 Rossi raised the cathedral-like
structure to the third and fourth floors, during what Morgan
called the "big pour," and by 1924 he extended it high enough
to reveal the "Ronda" towers that Hearst and Morgan had
conceived of back in 1919.

Despite his protracted absence from San Simeon, Hearst
had kept abreast of the work with his customary thoroughness.
The project had long since assumed a complexity that charac-
terized all his endeavors, a multiplicity that challenged his
vibrant imagination and nearly foolproof memory. Countless
architectural questions along with matters ranging from road-
work and fencing to water and power supplies had been
submitted to him by Julia Morgan and, as often, to her by
Hearst. Now a man of sixty, Hearst would live almost thirty
more years, through at least half of which he would enjoy
vigorous health. Surely with the houses virtually completed
and the main building well under way, his mind was humming
with visions of grandeur, his spirit animated by the great
enterprise unfolding before him.

One aspect of the project that Hearst had been thinking
about from early on was that of landscape design, planting
schemes, and horticulture. Late in 1920 he arrranged through a
nursery in Santa Barbara for the first shipment of plants to San
Simeon. The building site remained devoid of any but native
flora, most notably the great coast live oaks, until the Santa

Barbara shipment was planted in 1921. This modest beginning foreshadowed the eventual character of the gardens, which Mrs. Fremont Older related were inspired by those on the estate of Hearst's grandparents near Alviso in the Santa Clara Valley. Most of the early landscaping was concentrated near the three houses, which, unlike the emerging main building, lent themselves to a liberal use of plants in their courtyards and along their exterior walls and terraces. The houses, in fact, were briefly known as Casa Rosa, Casa Bougainvillea, and Casa Heliotrope.

Hearst had also cast his eyes on the mostly treeless slopes "outside the wall"—on the areas beyond the immediate architectural group. In 1922, through George C. Roeding's California Nursery Company in Niles, near San Jose, he and Julia Morgan recruited Nigel Keep, an English plantsman of the old school who had trained under Roeding, one of the leading nurserymen in the country. Keep, who at first filled in briefly as head gardener "inside the wall," had been hired for a much more ambitious task—the development of orchards and the forestation of dozens of acres of barren slopes on adjoining Lone Tree Hill and elsewhere on the ranch. Nigel Keep worked at San Simeon for more than twenty years, during which he and Hearst became close friends. Others who figured at various times in the landscape and horticultural work were Gardner Dailey, who later became a leading architect in the Bay Area; the artist Bruce Porter of San Francisco; the horticulturist Isabella Worn, also of San Francisco; and the landscape architect Charles Gibbs Adams of Los Angeles, who enjoyed a flourishing practice in Southern California. (The late Pete Sebastian, who worked for several years in the gardens, remembered Adams as something of a "wise guy." In 1940 the *Saturday Evening Post* published an article by Adams, who was ungallant enough to describe Julia Morgan as "a prim, wrinkled, vigorous little old lady" and misinformed enough to claim that "she had been taken to Paris as a girl by Mrs. Phoebe

Hearst to study and be a companion for Mrs. Hearst's boy, William." The article drew a rare letter of protest from the publicity-shunning Miss Morgan.) In the long run William Randolph Hearst and Julia Morgan were the minds behind San Simeon's landscape architecture. Masterpieces like the palm-lined Esplanade surrounding the main building and the winding pergola on Lone Tree Hill are their joint legacy more than anyone else's. Hearst and Morgan were fellow landscape architects, just as much as they were fellow architects of buildings.

Another aspect of the project that had engaged Hearst's attention since 1919 was that of collecting art, especially art for San Simeon. Hearst had been a familiar figure in the art world since the 1890s, often collecting for pleasure as an "amateur," along with other auction-room sportsmen of the day. Most of his purchases before 1919 went into the Clarendon, his huge apartment on Riverside Drive in New York. And now there was San Simeon to give Hearst a new focus, a new need—and a mighty inheritance to give him a new means. Once he and Julia Morgan agreed on a Spanish theme in 1919, he began to collect complementary items through the New York art market. At the opening of the 1919-20 sales season, New York's galleries were laden with hand-me-downs of every description imported from the Old World; Spanish items were especially in evidence, as were equally suitable Italian ones. Even more furnishings, more objects of art, more architectural elements became available to wealthy Americans as the twen-

Hearst was not only a collector of art objects and architectural elements but a collector of exotic animals as well. He began bringing in animals for San Simeon's zoo in the mid-1920s. At its height in the 1930s the zoo included dozens of grazing species, such as zebras, on the open slopes above the coastal plain. Still other animals were housed closer to the Enchanted Hill itself in enclosures designed by Julia Morgan.

ties unfolded. The diversity and abundance proved nearly inexhaustible—a bonanza that history timed perfectly for William Randolph Hearst.

From 1919 until the mid-1920s, when he began spending most of his time in California, Hearst followed the market firsthand and with more determination than ever before, often spending several hours a week in the auction rooms and galleries. He collected on a spectacular scale, stockpiling art and architectural works in grandiose array for his new dream house. He covered the European market at the same time through agents in London and on the Continent; although New York now dominated the market, there were still prizes to be bagged abroad, choice things that would probably never be available in this country. No other American was better represented in Europe.

(It has often been said that one of Hearst's purposes in building San Simeon—perhaps even his chief purpose—was to house a group of objects he had already collected. No such claim was made by Mrs. Fremont Older, who referred only to Hearst's initial desire in 1919 to have buildings suitable for "his large collection of Indian rugs," by which she may have meant his Navajo and Mexican textiles. The idea—or rather the fallacy—of Hearst's waiting in the wings with a collection earmarked for San Simeon apparently stems most of all from *Citizen Hearst,* in which W. A. Swanberg concluded that Hearst had wanted to build "his dream castle at San Simeon" long before 1919. Swanberg may have misinterpreted Mrs. Older's clues as well as other evidence; other writers have done likewise, though none with more conviction—or more lasting influence. Hearst "could not yet build his castle, a delay that gnawed at him," Swanberg wrote, "so the next best thing was to buy the decorations that would make it what he intended it to be, the most beautiful place in the world." The idea persists today, although the Julia Morgan Collection and related documentation have left it with fewer and fewer adherents. Above all, it is a fallacy to assume that Hearst needed clearly defined goals before embarking on the pursuit of his dream; he developed the scenario once he actually began. As Mrs. Older said, Hearst at the outset "had little conception whither his sense of beauty, knowledge of art and passion for perfection would lead.")

By March 1920, Hearst had accumulated enough material to fill a freight car, which he dispatched to California in time for Julia Morgan to incorporate some of the architectural pieces in the three houses. From then until the late 1930s, several "carloads," as these rail shipments were designated in Hearst's records, were sent from New York to the west coast each year. At first for Morgan they seemed like Christmas one moment and a burden the next. But Hearst became more purposeful in his buying, and Morgan became more adept at working with his acquisitions; for both of them the art collection asssumed greater importance, though not to the exclusion of other matters, such as the craftsmen's work, the landscaping, or the providing of accommodations for family members and guests. As Julia Morgan explained when she wrote in 1921 to the antiquarians Arthur Byne and Mildred Stapley Byne, who were soon to be purveyors of Spanish art to Hearst direct from their home base in Madrid: "We are building for him a sort of village on a mountain-top overlooking the sea and ranges and ranges of mountains, miles from any railway, and housing, incidentally, his collection as well as his family." The larger, total view of what Hearst and Morgan were attempting at San Simeon was always to be borne in mind.

In another letter of 1921 to the Bynes in Madrid, Julia Morgan described the results of Hearst's collecting to date:

> So far we have received from him, to incorporate in the new buildings, some twelve or thirteen carloads of antiques, brought from the ends of the earth and from prehistoric down to the late Empire in period, the majority, however, being of Spanish origin.

They comprise vast quantities of tables, beds, armoires, secretaires, all kinds of cabinets, polychrome church statuary, columns, door frames, carved doors in all stages of repair and disrepair, over-altars, reliquaries, lanterns, iron grille doors, window grilles, votive candlesticks, torcheres, all kinds of chairs in quantity, six or seven well heads (only one of these Spanish), marble and wood columns and door trims, a few good wooden carved ceilings, one very nice gilt and polychrome ceiling hexagonal in shape, one very fine rejere [grille] about 18′ wide and 17′ high, a marble sanctuary arch from the entrance to some choir, and pictures,—most of these of early type painted on wood, with a few good canvases; a number of Donatellos, lots of Della Robbias. I don't see myself where we are ever going to use half [of these items] suitably, but I find that the idea is to try things out and if they are not satisfactory, discard them for the next thing that comes that promises better. There is interest and charm coming gradually into play.

The collection Hearst had rapidly been adding to since 1919 had become a thing of increasing fascination and significance by the time he began using San Simeon more extensively in the mid-1920s, no less so for Julia Morgan than for Hearst himself. In 1924 Morgan revealed to Arthur Byne how much she had come to share in this aspect of Hearst's ever-expanding dream when she wrote, "I have developed an absorptive

San Simeon was destined to be more than just a museum of art objects. The buildings and grounds Hearst and Morgan were creating, dominated by the cathedral-like Casa Grande, were themselves destined to be the components of an architectural museum, the fulfillment of Hearst's conception of a "harmonious whole." But for the time being, through the rest of the 1920s and on into the 1930s, Casa Grande and the outlying houses had another role to play—that of buildings accommodating Hearst and his varied entourage as comfortably as possible.

capacity that seems ungodly when I stop to reflect." And in March 1925 Morgan told Byne that if he could get "finer and more important things they would be welcome." Two years later, on February 19, 1927, Hearst expressed the same view in one of the most memorable passages in his extensive correspondence with Julia Morgan:

> A great many very fine things will be arriving for the ranch—some of them have already arrived.
>
> They are for the most part of a much higher grade than we have had heretofore. In fact, I have decided to buy only the finest things for the ranch from now on, and we will probably weed out some of our less desirable articles.
>
> I had no idea when we began to build the ranch that I would be here so much or that the construction itself would be so important. Under the present circumstances, I see no reason why the ranch should not be a museum of the best things that I can secure.

This was Hearst's first reference to San Simeon as a museum, but in all likelihood he and Morgan had already considered it one, perhaps for quite some time. In any event, they set their sights accordingly, prompting Walter Steilberg to speak of them years later as "long distance dreamers" who were "looking way, way ahead."

The museum idea had a practical, immediate side too. With Hearst's life revolving more and more around San Simeon, and with his reputation as the perfect host firmly established in New York and Hollywood, why shouldn't he make his hilltop palace as magnificent as possible? Why shouldn't he create a backdrop that would dazzle and amaze today and that would enrich and inspire tomorrow? Hearst, the great dreamer, the consummate showman, knew that if he proceeded accordingly he would not be playing to an empty house.

Hearst at Home

I N THE mid-1920s William Randolph Hearst spent more time at the ranch than he had before, and he increasingly did so from then on. In its lengthy 1931 feature "Hearst at Home," *Fortune* magazine noted that Mr. Hearst had spent 204 days in residence at San Simeon during 1930, something that would have been unimaginable ten years earlier. (Half the remaining days in 1930 Hearst devoted to a European excursion; the other half he divided between New York and Los Angeles.) By 1930 La Cuesta Encantada had become Hearst's favorite and most frequented address, and it remained so for the next ten years. The estate had also become the favorite of the many guests who enjoyed Hearst's kingly hospitality, if only for a fleeting weekend. For them La Cuesta Encantada was a wonderland that fully lived up to its name.

Hearst was an indulgent host, even during the camping days of the late 1910s. The Camp Hill of that period consisted of a main dining tent and a cluster of smaller bedroom and service tents; that arrangement, along with traditions like the screening of movies under the spacious California sky, foreshadowed the marvels to come. Julia Morgan knew from early on that, by replacing the tents with permanent buildings, Hearst intended to accommodate and entertain not only himself and his family but many others as well. The idea of an architectural group consisting of a main building and outlying houses made that intention plain to see. But the thought of providing for guests in a truly grand manner probably had yet to occur to either of them. Like everything else in the San Simeon epic, the social history began modestly. A decade later the transformation was well along, and in its 1931 article *Fortune* could report that for most of the 204 days in 1930 Hearst had "kept his guest rooms fairly full, the court being in session." *Fortune* also mentioned that some of the recent guests had been as noteworthy as Winston Churchill, who had visited San Simeon in September 1929.

But the names of only a few guests from the earliest years are known. Undoubtedly they were newspapermen, business and political associates, family friends, theater and motion picture people, and others both renowned and obscure—a prelude to the social makeup that is better documented from the mid-1920s on. In 1924, for instance—or perhaps in 1925—the author Adela Rogers St. Johns apparently visited the ranch for the first time; she described the experience in her autobiography, *The Honeycomb,* beginning with an account of her ride up from Los Angeles one night with Hearst:

"We went into a roadside diner at Los Alamos and sat on stools and Mr. Hearst said he recommended the ham and eggs *or* the chili so I had both. Then we got back on the road. Coming out of San Luis Obispo, where we took Coast Highway 1 by Morro Bay instead of the inland route to Paso Robles and the Salinas Valley, we ran into a sort of cold corn-soup fog, clammy and cream-yellow, which thickened so the car had to cut it like a knife. We were on a one-lane in each direction dirt road with no lights, no white lines, our car lights were dim. The sea was on one side, a cliff high on the other. . . . Our driver hung his head out though what good he thought that was going to do him I don't know. Then Mr. Hearst said gently, 'Here is a shoulder, pull off and I will drive.' . . .

"...I have never witnessed such uncanny mechanical manipulation as Mr. Hearst's driving that night.

"Fifty miles to San Simeon. Though from time to time I heard a car or the rocks bouncing down from the cliff edge, I never saw anything. Our way was as wide as the car's wheels, no wider, and as spiral as a corkscrew. We drove at a steady, fast pace, once or twice we stopped to let a gate swing open under the invisible guidance of a Mexican cowboy....

"From that day to this I have been sure that, whatever his faults, Mr. Hearst could see in the dark."

Another visitor in 1924—in this instance the date is certain—was John F. Hylan, the mayor through whom William Randolph Hearst exerted potent influence on the municipal affairs of New York City.

In 1924 a new era began at San Simeon. Until then Hearst's visits had usually been family activities that originated in New York, required a fair amount of planning, favored the summer months, and involved small groups of guests. But in 1924 his visits became more frequent, were often short trips made any time of year, sometimes at the drop of a hat, and were more inclined to favor Hollywood celebrities—those "wild movie people," as he said to Julia Morgan. Some new developments in Hearst's life made 1924 a turning point. Mr. and Mrs. Hearst were in the midst of separating, and Hearst had begun spending much of his time in Los Angeles, where his Cosmopolitan Productions—featuring Marion Davies as the principal star—had found a new home under the wing of Metro-Goldwyn-Mayer in Culver City. The Metro crowd included many of the Hollywood elite. Louis B. Mayer, Greta Garbo, John Gilbert, Norma Shearer, Irving Thalberg, and other greats of the silent era soon bestowed an aura of glamour on San Simeon that became legendary. Another Hollywood notable who journeyed up the coast was Rudolph Valentino, whose death in 1926 denied him the experience of Hearst's kingdom at its zenith. The mystique of Valentino lingers in the little town of Harmony, which fondly remembers that he and Pola Negri stopped at its roadside creamery during a trip to the ranch.

The three houses were virtually complete by 1924, but no more than temporary or improvised use could be made of the main building. Hearst himself maintained quarters in the largest house, by then named Casa del Mar. The two others, Casa del Sol and Casa del Monte, provided a total of twelve bedrooms. If filled to capacity, along with whatever guest space was available in Casa del Mar, the houses could accommodate about twenty-five people. When the main building came into use during the late 1920s, space opened up for about fifteen more. But not until the 1930s did Casa Grande swell to the immense size we see today—a piecemeal evolution achieved partly through the addition of still more guest suites. (The tendency for years has been to call the three houses "guest houses." The term appeared early in the literature of San Simeon, although Hearst and Morgan themselves seem almost never to have used it. Evidently "house" was for them a simple descriptive term with more of an architectural than a social connotation, as was "main building" with its variants "main house," "big house," and the like. The main building eventually contained more guest rooms than the houses combined did.) Only then could Hearst accommodate fifty or sixty—a number

William Randolph Hearst had always been a dreamer,
both in building his publishing empire and in building his
great houses, the greatest of which was San Simeon. He
had always been an accomplished host, too. With the three
houses completed and the main building well under way,
Hearst could use the estate more often and could entertain
increasing numbers of guests. San Simeon eventually
became his most frequented residence, the one he
preferred using during the fall through spring—a marked
departure from the old camping days, when he had used
San Simeon exclusively during the summer.

still far from the exaggerated claims, deeply ingrained in San Simeon mythology, of 100 or even 150. (Some very large groups were in fact entertained for lunch or dinner, but not everyone stayed overnight on those occasions.) We need not be disappointed by the more realistic figures of one or two dozen guests with increases at times to double that number or slightly more. Even as few a five or ten people could be enough to make San Simeon exciting and colorful.

Just such a group was at the ranch in December 1925, on this occasion Mr. and Mrs. Hearst and their five sons, who by now ranged from ten years of age to twenty-one. The Refectory, the dining room in Casa Grande, was not yet ready for use. So the Hearst family had Christmas Eve dinner in the adjoining Assembly Room, which was itself partly unfinished but already impressively decorated. Short stays were still the rule in 1925; the Hearsts soon left the ranch, though not before Mrs. Hearst treated some of the local children to a party on Christmas Day. Mr. Hearst, meanwhile, continued to stay in Casa del Mar during his intermittent visits until at least the latter part of 1927, after which his private Gothic Suite in Casa Grande was ready for use.

La Cuesta Encantada was on the verge of its heyday by 1927. But one obstacle stood in the way, an old nemesis actually—the weather. No one builds high in the Santa Lucias without courting nature's occasional wrath. Summer poses its threat of fire, winter its swollen creeks and mudslides. Hearst and his guests might enjoy tennis and riding during a balmy mid-winter period—a mesmerizing calm before the storm—only to be pounded a few days later by a frontal system sweeping full force down the California coast. Twice as much rain falls at 1,600 feet as on the coastal plain, sometimes more. And the wind that often accompanies a big storm! Tiles are blown from roofs, branches from trees, and people very nearly from their feet. Hearst was at the ranch in February 1927 when some ferocious weather set in. "I have never seen anything as severe as the onslaught of these storms," he wrote to Julia Morgan on February 19. "The only thing I can liken them to is a storm at sea, and I think we should provide against this onslaught just as we would provide on a boat against a storm at sea, with extraordinarily heavy protections."

This was the same letter, ironically, in which Hearst first spoke of San Simeon as a museum. Two weeks earlier Hearst had written to Camille Rossi, the resident construction superintendent, "Let's have COMFORT AND HEALTH before so much art. The art won't do us any good if we are all dead of pneumonia." On February 16, at the height of the stormy weather, Hearst again wrote to Rossi:

> We are all leaving the hill. We are drowned, blown and frozen out. The trouble is not merely with the weather. It is with the *houses*.
>
> In the various rooms of the small houses the weather strips wail like a chorus of lost souls, the windows leak little rivers of running water and under the doors the cold draughts blow like thin hurricanes until the rugs flop on the floor.
>
> Everybody has a cold. All who could [leave] have left and the few who remain are eagerly waiting a chance to get out.
>
> . . . If we are to live in these houses we *must* make them fit to live in. Before we build anything more let's make what we have built practical, comfortable and beautiful. If we can't do that we might as well change the names of the houses to pneumonia house, diptheria house and influenza bungalow. The main house we can call the clinic.

He also wrote to Julia Morgan, "We had a lively time in house A [Casa del Mar] last night. The storm was severe and I spent most of the night ripping off the weather stripping in my room. The darn stuff sounded like a flock of saxophones going at full tilt in a jazz band." Hearst had had no idea when he began to build San Simeon that he would be there "so much or that the construction itself would be so important"; he also had had no idea that San Simeon would become increasingly a winter residence. Under the circumstances some "extraordinarily heavy protections" were indeed warranted. Before returning to Los Angeles, Hearst left Rossi with detailed instructions on how to proceed and said, "I am not coming back to the hill until we put the small houses at least on a livable basis."

When finally equipped with heavier windows, dovetailed weather stripping, and a better heating system, the buildings enabled Hearst to begin truly enjoying the fruits of nearly ten years' work, rain or shine. The heyday was in full swing by the end of the 1920s and lasted about ten years, during which the most memorable guests in San Simeon's social history visited the ranch. In addition to Hollywood celebrities, there were notables such as Charles Lindbergh, who flew up from Los Angeles one weekend while on his nationwide tour in the summer of 1927. (Hearst, a longtime proponent of aviation, had sponsored the historic Dominguez Air Meet in Los Angeles in 1910 and had recently begun flying into San Simeon in a Fokker airplane. He later owned a Stinson and a Vultee.) Jimmy Walker, mayor of New York City, was a standout in 1928. Winston Churchill was easily the most prominent guest in 1929. An airborne visitor in 1929 was the *Graf Zeppelin,* whose world flight Hearst sponsored. L. "Whistle" McAninch, a driver for Steve's Taxi, the chauffeur service operated by Steve Zegar of San Luis Obispo, noted in his log for August 25 that the famous dirigible passed over San Simeon at 9:37 P.M. Ex-President Calvin Coolidge stayed for a week in the winter of 1930; Hearst staged a formal dinner in his honor, a rare event at the informal ranch. Another guest in 1930 was the novelist Theodore Dreiser, who lunched with Hearst and discussed the case of the wrongfully imprisoned radical Tom Mooney, in whose behalf Fremont Older, one of Hearst's top editors, had been crusading since 1918 in the *San Francisco Call-Bulletin.*

Hearst's editors and executives were frequent guests. In

addition to legendary figures like Fremont Older, Walter Howey, and Eleanor Patterson there was Arthur Brisbane, whose front-page column "Today" was read by millions. Writing occasionally under the dateline "Hearst Ranch, San Simeon, Calif.," Brisbane gave the public some of its earliest glimpses of Hearst's fabled estate. In his column for February 9, 1930, Brisbane described the ride to the ranch from San Luis Obispo, where he had arrived at 2:15 A.M. on the Southern Pacific Lark from Los Angeles: " 'Whistle' McAninch, who drives the big Packard car for Steve Zegar, says: 'No fog, so we can do sixty nicely.' This is to reassure you. He does seventy nicely, telling you that the cows do not get on the road as much as they used to do, and anyhow, with the moon, you can see them." Seventy miles an hour! And to think a mere eight years had passed since Julia Morgan wrote of the bone-jarring conditions between Cayucos and Cambria!

Brisbane, in his column for March 1, 1931, was probably the first to describe a dramatic episode in the construction that has since been recounted many times:

"Tree moving—important to the beautifying of the earth, has been highly developed on this ranch by C.C. Rossi, engineer.

"After experts had said it was impossible to move certain enormous live oak trees, because of their great age and size, Mr. Rossi moved them, including one at least a thousand years old, covering about an acre with its shade.

"It was transplanted five years ago, and is thriving, as are several others, almost as big.... With the tree was moved a plot of earth forty feet in diameter, nine feet deep. Around this earth plot was built a 'tub' of concrete, forty feet wide. The staves [were] made of separate concrete blocks, held together by heavy bands of iron.

"Tunnelling under the earth, the soil and roots were supported from below by a criss-cross of concrete beams. The total weight moved, with powerful jacks, exceeded six hundred tons.

It cost five thousand dollars to move one tree a few hundred feet, but such a tree is worth the money, if you have the five thousand dollars."

Two oaks were moved in this manner in 1926—although on a less stupendous scale than Brisbane described—to make way for the Theater and its surmounting Recreation Wing. These additions to the north side of Casa Grande were not begun, however, until 1929. Whereas remoteness and primitive conditions caused delays in the early years, now the sheer size and diversity of the project frequently did so. A backlog of unfinished work accumulated.

As the project entered its second decade, the future looked both promising and discouraging. On the one hand there was the momentum that several years' effort had generated; there was also the experience that everyone involved had gained and contributed—both of which factors made Hearst closer to the realization of his dream. On the other hand there was the Depression, which was tightening its grip on the country—even a man of Hearst's great wealth and power was affected. Had the prosperity of the 1920s continued, Hearst would still have tried to complete San Simeon. Many once believed—especially in the absence of documentation like the Julia Morgan Collection—that he had no intention of finishing the

Mature trees were often used in transforming the California landscape of the 1920s, but seldom on the scale attempted at San Simeon with Italian cypresses, Canary Island palms, and even native oaks. A few massive oaks, each weighing tons when encased in a concrete "flower pot," were moved by Camille Rossi and his crew. Despite Rossi's dismissal as superintendent in 1932, his knowledge of tree moving was invaluable, and he returned to San Simeon in 1946 to help move another great oak behind the main building. By then Rossi's previous efforts had been immortalized by Arthur Brisbane in his column of March 3, 1931.

project, that he would have built and rebuilt and tinkered and altered indefinitely, with no particular regard for the outcome. But his intentions were more coherent, more purposeful than they may have seemed to many observers. So were Julia Morgan's. In June 1934 she wrote to Arthur Byne, through whom Hearst was still collecting Spanish art, "On account of conditions, work has gone along very slowly on the Hill. . . . I hope a 'pick-up' is really coming and that next year will let us make some appearance of finish to at least parts long years under way." Morgan clearly was as committed as Hearst was to making San Simeon the "harmonious whole" that Hearst had spoken of as early as 1919. Morgan was likewise committed to San Simeon's potential as a museum. "Of course, this is just temporary for his use," she once told Walter Steilberg. "The country needs architectural museums, not just places where you hang paintings and sculptures."

Keeping these goals as well as more practical considerations in mind, Hearst and Morgan soon completed Hearst's private Gothic Study and the spectacular Neptune Pool through George Loorz, who had replaced Camille Rossi in 1932. But an equally spectacular feature never got past the conceptual stage—the revised scheme Hearst had recently proposed for the back of Casa Grande. On April 26, 1932, Hearst described to Julia Morgan an idea he thought "should provide the crowning glory" of the hilltop:

> Instead of having the rotunda east of the patio which we had contemplated, to have a great ballroom and banqueting hall, which shall extend from one wing to the other and completely enclose the patio.
>
> This room would be 150 feet long and would contain eight great Gothic tapestries. . . .
>
> Opposite the entrance we could put our big reredos, if that is what they call the thing. . . .
>
> The hall should be about the height of the refectory, and should be lighted by windows from the top. . . .

Byne is just sending us a great ceiling, something over a hundred feet long, and we could piece this out a bit at either end.

I am asking Brummer [the art dealer] to get those French flamboyant Gothic fireplaces, one to go at either end of the hall.

I think this can be made the grandest hall in America. . . .

When this hall is not in use as a ballroom or banqueting hall, it could be used to contain some of the important collections in [display] cases in the middle of the room. We could also use a lot of armor there. . . .

That is the scheme!

Isn't it a pippin?

Hearst signed his letter, "Your assistant architect"; Morgan replied by telegram, with equal enthusiasm, "It certainly will be a marvelous room as you say a pippin." For the next two years the idea of a Great Hall enlivened their correspondence and inspired sketches and drawings, but actual construction never began.

All the while, greater San Simeon felt the presence of William Randolph Hearst, whose dream was manifested by more than his hilltop palace alone. The warehouses and residences he built in the town of San Simeon, the improvements he made on Rancho Piedra Blanca, the acreage he added to his inherited holdings, with which additions he extended his boundaries up to Pacific Valley and inland to encompass the old land grants surrounding Jolon and Mission San Antonio—all were manifestations of his kingly nature, his instinct for grandeur, his quest for empire. At Jolon he and Julia Morgan built the Milpitas Hacienda, which served as headquarters for his ranch operations in Monterey County during the 1930s. Today Milpitas is part of Fort Hunter Liggett and is still mistaken by travelers for the nearby mission. Hearst and his party sometimes rode horseback from San Simeon to Milpitas, crossing the Santa Lucias to the Nacimiento River, where they intercepted the route taken by Gaspar de Portola in 1769 and 1770.

Hearst's dream had still another manifestation—the collection of animals he began assembling in the 1920s, entire herds of which roamed freely in a 2,000-acre preserve on the slopes of La Cuesta Encantada. Though most were exotic species, Hearst had an abiding interest in common ones as well, as Mrs. Fremont Older related. "A statesman or celebrity may bore him," she wrote, "but his face lights up with tenderness when a young spotted deer breaks away from her herd as Bessie does, and at sunset clatters up the tiled terraces of San Simeon. When Diana, the seal, came into port at San Simeon, waddled up to the warehouses and decided to adopt the ranch as her home, Hearst was as pleased as if a distinguished visitor had arrived from Mars. For the moment he abandoned national and international interests, and set his mind to work on Diana's future. By telephone he ordered a shelter to be made for her so that daily she might be fed fresh fish, and at the same time have a daily plunge in the Pacific. Soon Diana became so tame that she tried to live in the house of her keeper." It logically follows that Hearst was an unrelenting foe of vivisection and cruelty to animals, both of which were the subjects of ongoing crusades in his chain of newspapers.

Hearst was no less sympathetic toward his fellow man, especially on the local level. Pete Sebastian, whose historic

The affable George Loorz replaced the fiery Camille Rossi as construction superintendent in 1932. Loorz, building methodically upon Rossi's ten years on the job, worked closely with Mr. Hearst and Miss Morgan to finish several important projects over the next six years, among them the Billiard Room, the Duplex Suites, Hearst's Gothic Study, and both swimming pools. The drawing here is based on a photograph of Loorz taken near the Egyptian sculptures of the goddess Sekhmet, San Simeon's most ancient art objects.

store in San Simeon is still operating after more than a century, never tired of recollecting how Hearst, during the dreariest years of the Depression, authorized him to distribute fifty dollars' worth of provisions each month to struggling families in the area. As many as forty-five or fifty families, scattered from San Simeon Creek to Ragged Point, were the beneficiaries from about 1932 to 1934. Sebastian forwarded the monthly bills to the *San Francisco Examiner*. Without Hearst's generosity and patronage Sebastian himself might well have gone under during those years, to say nothing of the families Hearst helped support.

Hearst continued to build and to entertain as much as he could. San Simeon provided the most enviable social experience of the era, not only for the Hollywood crowd but also for a great array of other notable people. George Bernard Shaw, for example, arrived in March 1933 for what was supposedly his only overnight stay in a private residence in this country. J. Paul Getty's signature appears in Hearst's guest book under the date of January 7, 1935. Later that year, H.G. Wells, who was in Hollywood while the movie *Things to Come* was being adapted from his futuristic novel, visited the ranch in the company of Charlie Chaplin and Paulette Goddard. Three years later the sculptor of Mount Rushmore, Gutzon Borglum, paid a visit; his name appears in the guest book alongside David Niven's. Among the Hollywood guests were also the directors, actors, scenarists, and others in the film colony who worked on the Marion Davies pictures, the last of which was made in 1937. In addition, three of Hearst's sons—George, William, Jr., and John—who were now grown and were working in the Hearst organization, were frequent guests; they also accompanied their father on his sojourn in Europe in 1934. Though Hearst was in his seventies he was as fun-loving as people many years younger. Costume parties were a particular favorite, especially on the twenty-ninth of April, his birthday. For entertainment the Sons of the Pioneers, featuring Leonard

Slye (who later became Roy Rogers), were as appropriate as the ketchup bottles that graced the dining tables à la Camp Hill. Could anything have been more amusing than the sight of the Sons of the Pioneers, who were mostly rank greenhorns, when on one occasion they had to pack their big bass fiddle and other gear into one of Hearst's backcountry campsites on San Carpoforo Creek?

Always keen on enhancing San Simeon—on making the "harmonious whole" as harmonious as possible—Hearst wrote to Julia Morgan from Rome in the summer of 1936 during his final trip to Europe:

> One thing which San Simeon really needs is fountains.
> I mean fountains which *fount.*...
> After seeing the Villa D'Este again I realize what water would do for San Simeon. It would double its beauty and charm. In the midst of a dry land we would have an oasis of beautiful fountains. The work must be done on a grand scale and there must not be merely statuary and basins but *water*—spouting, tumbling water.

But the Depression wore on, and Hearst's proposed fountains went the way of his Great Hall when construction was finally halted in 1937. Expenses had to be cut drastically; capital had to be generated to save Hearst's empire. Certain newspapers and magazines were sold or merged; most of the other components of Hearst's vast holdings were at least partially liquidated; the collecting of art was abandoned entirely, and much of the surplus was sold. Somehow construction resumed briefly in 1938 with a very small crew, but after that the job shut down completely.

Hearst also had to trim his living expenses. Wyntoon, the Tyrolean summer retreat he had been developing near Mount Shasta throughout the 1930s, provided a more economical alternative to San Simeon. Despite its snowbound winters, Wyntoon became virtually a year-round residence for Hearst and his entourage from about 1940 until nearly the end of the Second World War. San Simeon was all but boarded up, with a skeleton crew left behind as caretakers. From deep in the Cascades, alongside the McCloud River, Hearst directed his newspapers, his magazines, his radio stations, and his other holdings—their numbers now reduced but still great—just as he had from San Simeon. In 1943 he turned eighty.

The Hearst empire recovered substantially during the war, fueled by the strong economy. By 1944 Hearst was able to resume construction at Wyntoon, even to resume collecting on a modest scale. And with better days in sight, his dream once more was of San Simeon; he returned there late that year. "We must finish the job," W. A. Swanberg recounted Hearst's having told his cousin Randolph Apperson, the manager of Rancho Piedra Blanca. In the fall of 1945, under Maurice McClure, the new construction superintendent, a big crew resumed work for the first time in several years. But apparently there was no thought of building anything as grandiose as the Great Hall; instead the postwar work revolved around the enlargement and completion of the Recreation Wing, now called the New Wing, on which the last flurries of construction in 1937 and 1938 had been concentrated. Other work was done in the opposite Service Wing of Casa Grande and in Casa del Mar, where

Hearst bought portions of an ancient temple from Galleria Sangiorgi in Rome in 1922. From then until the Neptune Pool was completed in the mid-1930s, the temple ensemble figured in his plans for San Simeon. To complement the temple, Julia Morgan designed two Vermont marble pavilions, one of them visible here at the south end of the pool. And to enhance the setting further, the Parisian sculptor Charles Cassou was commissioned to produce the white marble groups flanking the temple at poolside. Familiar now to millions around the world, the Neptune Pool has become an enduring symbol of Hearst's dream.

Hearst lived during his last two and a half years at the ranch. The crew also built an airstrip on the coastal plain large enough for Hearst's new DC-3C. Warren McClure, Julia Morgan's assistant on various Hearst projects since 1929, was now the acting architect.

Failing health forced Hearst to move to Beverly Hills in 1947, soon after his eighty-fourth birthday. Warren McClure and Maurice McClure (who were unrelated) continued working on the New Wing, completing it in 1948. Construction stopped once more, this time for good. In Hearst's protracted absence the estate reverted to the care of a minimal staff, which was alerted on more than one occasion that Mr. Hearst would soon be coming back. But though mentally keen and still in control of his great empire, he never returned. Thus Hearst's pursuit of his dream ended quietly. He truly had gone full circle.

Hearst died in 1951. He was buried alongside his parents at Cypress Lawn Cemetery near San Francisco, the city of his birth. The journey from San Francisco in 1863, to New York in 1895, back to California in the mid-1920s, and finally back to his birthplace in 1951 was an eighty-eight-year odyssey for William Randolph Hearst. It remains one of the most remarkable odysseys in American history, all the more so for what he and Julia Morgan created—San Simeon, their legacy that endures today as Hearst San Simeon State Historical Monument.

BIBLIOGRAPHY

Adams, Charles Gibbs. "Gardens for the Stars." *Saturday Evening Post* (March 2, 1940): 18-19; 71-74

Aidala, Thomas R. *Hearst Castle: San Simeon.* New York: Hudson Hills Press, 1981.

Angel, Myron. *History of San Luis Obispo County, California, with Illustrations and Biographical Sketches of Its Prominent Men and Pioneers.* Oakland: Thompson & West, 1883.

Bancroft, Hubert Howe. *California Pastoral: 1769-1848.* San Francisco: The History Company, 1888.

——. *History of California: 1542-1890.* Seven volumes. San Francisco: The History Company, 1886-90.

Bean, Walton. *California: An Interpretive History.* New York: McGraw-Hill Book Company, 1968.

Berkeley. H. C. Forney Papers. In the private possession of Mrs. H. C. Forney and her daughter, Lynn Forney Stone.

Best, Gerald M. *Ships and Narrow Gauge Rails: The Story of the Pacific Coast Company.* Berkeley: Howell-North Books, 1964.

Bidlack, Russell E., ed. "To California on the Sarah Sands: Two Letters Writen in 1850 by L.R. Slawson." *California Historical Society Quarterly* (September 1965): 229-35.

Blomberg, Nancy J. *Navajo Textiles: The William Randolph Hearst Collection.* Tucson: The University of Arizona Press, 1988.

Bolton, Herbert Eugene. *Fray Juan Crespi: Missionary Explorer on the Pacific Coast 1769-1774.* Berkeley: University of California Press, 1927.

Bonfils, Winifred Black. *The Life and Personality of Phoebe Apperson Hearst.* San Francisco: John Henry Nash, 1928.

Boulian, Dorothy May. *Enchanted Gardens of Hearst Castle*. Cambria: Phildor Press, 1972.

Boutelle, Sara Holmes. *Julia Morgan: Architect*. New York: Abbeville Press, 1988.

Brisbane, Arthur. "Today." Syndicated newspaper column (February 9, 1930, and March 1, 1931).

Busch, Briton Cooper, ed. *Alta California 1840-1842: The Journal and Observations of William Dane Phelps, Master of the Ship "Alert."* Glendale: The Arthur H. Clark Company, 1983.

Byne, Arthur, and Mildred Stapley. *Spanish Architecture of the Sixteenth Century: General View of the Plateresque and Herrera Styles*. New York and London: G.P. Putnam's Sons, 1917.

Chapman, Charles E. *A History of California: The Spanish Period*. New York: The Macmillan Company, 1921.

Chase, J. Smeaton. *California Coast Trails: A Horseback Ride from Mexico to Oregon*. Boston and New York: Houghton Mifflin Company, 1913.

Cleland, Robert Glass. *A History of California: The American Period*. New York: The Macmillan Company, 1922.

Coffman, Taylor. *Hearst Castle: The Story of William Randolph Hearst and San Simeon*. Santa Barbara: Sequoia Communications, 1985.

____. *The William Randolph Hearst Collection*. San Luis Obispo: Tabula Rasa Press, 1987; Tabula Rasa Publications in Hearst Studies 1.

Collord, Marjorie, and Ann Miller. *The Enchanted Hill Cookbook: The Favorite Recipes of William Randolph Hearst with Rare Photos and Inside Glimpses of Hearst Castle and Its Celebrated Guests*. San Luis Obispo: Blake Printing & Publishing, 1985.

Cronise, Titus Fey. *The Natural Wealth of California*. San Francisco: H.H. Bancroft & Company, 1868.

Crowther, Bosley. *Hollywood Rajah: The Life and Times of Louis B. Mayer*. New York: Holt, Rinehart & Winston, 1960.

Descriptive Guide to the Julia Morgan Collection. San Luis Obispo: Department of Special Collections, Robert E. Kennedy Library, California Polytechnic State University, n.d. [1985].

Engelhardt, Zephyrin. *San Antonio de Padua: The Mission in the Sierras*. Santa Barbara: Mission Santa Barbara, 1929.

——. *San Miguel Arcangel: The Mission on the Highway.* Santa Barbara: Mission Santa Barbara, 1929.

Everingham, Carol J., comp. "Dateline: San Simeon 1919-1939: A Chronological Development of the Ideas, Plans, Drawings, and Actual Construction Starting in 1919 at the William Randolph Hearst Estate in San Simeon." Photocopied for private distribution. San Simeon, 1981.

Frey, Woody. "Making the Gardens at San Simeon." *Pacific Horticulture* (Fall 1978): 39-44.

Garnett, Porter. *Stately Homes of California.* Boston: Little, Brown & Company, 1915.

Gebhard, David, and Harriette Von Breton, eds. *Architecture in California 1868-1968.* Santa Barbara: The Art Galleries, University of California, Santa Barbara, 1968.

Gibson, Robert O. "Ethnogeography of the Salinan People: A Systems Approach." Master's thesis, California State University, Hayward, 1983.

Gudde, Erwin H. *California Place Names: A Geographical Dictionary.* Berkeley and Los Angeles: University of California Press, 1949.

Guiles, Fred Lawrence. *Marion Davies.* New York: McGraw-Hill Book Company, 1972.

Hamilton, Geneva. *Where the Highway Ends.* Cambria: Williams Printing Co., 1974.

Hanchett, Byron. *In and Around the Castle.* San Luis Obispo: Blake Publishing, 1985.

Hanna, Phil Townsend. *The Dictionary of California Land Names.* Los Angeles: The Automobile Club of Southern California, 1946.

Hearst, Mrs. William Randolph, Jr. *The Horses of San Simeon.* San Simeon: San Simeon Press, 1985.

"Hearst" [Wyntoon]. *Fortune* (October 1935): 42-55; 123-62.

"Hearst at Home." *Fortune* (May 1931): 56-68; 130.

Hines, Philip, et al. *The Prehistory of San Simeon Creek: 5800 B.P. to Missionization.* Sacramento: Department of Parks and Recreation, Resource Protection Division, 1986.

Holweck, F.G. *A Biographical Dictionary of the Saints: With a General Introduction on Hagiology.* St. Louis: B. Herder Book Co., 1924.

Jones, Mary Lou, et al., eds. *The Gray Whale: Eschrichtius robustus.* Orlando, Florida: Academic Press, 1984.

Kelsey, Harry. *Juan Rodriguez Cabrillo.* San Marino: The Huntington Library, 1986.

Krieger, Daniel E. *Looking Backward into the Middle Kingdom: San Luis Obispo County.* Northridge: Windsor Publications, 1988.

Kruckeberg, Henry W. *George Christian Roeding, 1868-1928. The Story of California's Leading Nurseryman and Fruit Grower.* Los Angeles: The California Association of Nurserymen, 1930.

Lewis, Oscar. *Fabulous San Simeon: A History of the Hearst Castle.* San Francisco: California Historical Society, 1958.

Loe, Nancy E. *William Randolph Hearst: An Illustrated Biography.* Santa Barbara: Sequoia Communications, 1988.

_____, ed. *San Simeon Revisited: The Correspondence Between Architect Julia Morgan and William Randolph Hearst.* San Luis Obispo: The Library Associates, California Polytechnic State University, 1987.

Longstreth, Richard. *Julia Morgan: Architect.* Berkeley: Berkeley Architectural Heritage Association, 1977.

Los Angeles. George Loorz Papers. In the private possession of the Loorz family.

MacKenzie, Norman and Jeanne. *H.G. Wells.* New York: Simon & Schuster, 1973.

MacShane, Frank. "The Romantic World of William Randolph Hearst." *The Centennial Review* (Summer 1964): 292-305.

Mathes, W. Michael. *Vizcaino and Spanish Expansion in the Pacific Ocean 1580-1630.* San Francisco: California Historical Society, 1968.

Miller, Bruce W. *Chumash: A Picture of Their World.* Los Osos: Sand River Press, 1988.

Mora, Jo. *Californios: The Saga of the Hard-riding Vaqueros, America's First Cowboys.* Garden City: Doubleday & Co., 1949.

Murray, Ken. *The Golden Days of San Simeon.* Garden City: Doubleday & Co., 1971.

Murray, Robert K. *The Harding Era: Warren G. Harding and His Administration.* Minneapolis: University of Minnesota Press, 1969.

Newton, A. Edward. "A Tourist in Spite of Himself—At the Hearst Ranch." *The Atlantic Monthly* (October 1932): 461-67.

Nicholson, Loren. *Rails Across the Ranchos.* Fresno: Valley Publishers, 1980.

Ogden, Adele. "Boston Hide Droghers Along California Shores." *California Historical Society Quarterly* (December 1929): 289-305.

——. *The California Sea Otter Trade 1784-1848.* Berkeley and Los Angeles: University of California Press, 1941.

——. "Hides and Tallow: McCulloch, Hartnell and Company 1822-1828." *California Historical Society Quarterly* (September 1927): 254-64.

Older, Mr. and Mrs. Fremont. *George Hearst: California Pioneer.* San Francisco: John Henry Nash, 1933.

Older, Mrs. Fremont. *William Randolph Hearst: American.* New York and London: D. Appleton-Century Company, 1936.

Pavlik, Robert C. "Christmas at the Castle." San Simeon: Hearst San Simeon State Historical Monument, 1988.

Pitt, Leonard. *The Decline of the Californios: A Social History of the Spanish-Speaking Californians, 1846-1890.* Berkeley: University of California Press, 1966.

Pomeroy, Earl. *In Search of the Golden West: The Tourist in Western America.* New York: Alfred A. Knopf, 1957.

Reinstedt, Randall A. *Gold in the Santa Lucias.* Carmel: Ghost Town Publications, 1973.

Riess, Suzanne B., et al., eds. *Julia Morgan Architectural History Project.* Two volumes. Berkeley: Regional Oral History Office, The Bancroft Library, University of California, 1976.

Roberts, Lois J., et al. *A Cultural Resources Reconnaissance and Overview: Fort Hunter Liggett, California.* Sacramento: Department of the Army, Sacramento District Corps of Engineers, 1979.

Robinson, Alfred. *Life in California.* Oakland: Biobooks, 1947.

Robinson, W.W. *Land in California: The Story of Mission Lands, Ranchos, Squatters, Mining Claims, Railroad Grants, Land Scrip, Homesteads.* Berkeley and Los Angeles: University of California Press, 1948.

——. *The Story of San Luis Obispo County.* Los Angeles: Title Insurance and Trust Company, 1957.

Rosten, Leo. *Hollywood: The Movie Colony, The Movie Makers.* New York: Harcourt, Brace & Co., 1941.

St. Johns, Adela Rogers. *The Honeycomb.* Garden City: Doubleday & Co., 1969.

Sanchez, Nellie Van de Grift. *Spanish and Indian Place Names of California: Their Meaning and Their Romance.* San Francisco: A.M. Robertson, 1914.

San Luis Obispo. Julia Morgan Collection. Special Collections and University Archives, Robert E. Kennedy Library, California Polytechnic State University.

San Simeon. Hearst San Simeon State Historical Monument Archives. San Simeon Region, California Department of Parks and Recreation.

Sarber, Jane, ed. *A Cabbie in a Golden Era: Featuring Cabbie's Original Log of Guests Transported to Hearst Castle.* Paso Robles: Privately published, 1982.

Squibb, Paul, ed. *Captain Portola in San Luis Obispo County in 1769.* Morro Bay: Tabula Rasa Press, 1984; San Luis Obispo County Heritage Series 1.

Starks, Edwin C. *A History of California Shore Whaling.* Sacramento: State of California Fish and Game Commission (Fish Bulletin No. 6), 1922.

Starr, Kevin. *Americans and the California Dream 1850-1915.* New York: Oxford University Press, 1973.

____. *Inventing the Dream: California Through the Progressive Era.* New York and Oxford: Oxford University Press, 1985.

Swanberg, W.A. *Citizen Hearst: A Biography of William Randolph Hearst.* New York: Charles Scribner's Sons, 1961.

____. *Dreiser.* New York: Charles Scribner's Sons, 1965.

Torre, Susana, ed. *Women in American Architecture: A Historic and Contemporary Perspective.* New York: Watson-Guptill Publications, 1977.

Towner, Wesley. *The Elegant Auctioneers.* New York: Hill & Wang, 1970.

"A Unique Tour of San Simeon." *Life* (August 26, 1957): 68-84.

Wagner, Henry Raup. *Juan Rodriguez Cabrillo: Discoverer of the Coast of California.* San Francisco: California Historical Society, 1941.

____. "Saints' Names in California." *Historical Society of Southern California Quarterly* (March 1947): 49-58.

____. *Spanish Voyages to the Northwest Coast of American in the*

Sixteenth Century. San Francisco: California Historical Society, 1929.

Watson, Douglas S. "Did the Chinese Discover America? A Critical Examination of the Buddhist Priest Hui Shen's Account of Fu Sang, and the Apocryphal Voyage of the Chinese Navigator Hee-Li." *California Historical Society Quarterly* (March 1935): 47-58.

Webb, Edith Buckland. *Indian Life at the Old Missions.* Los Angeles: W.F. Lewis, 1952.

Wells, Evelyn. *Fremont Older.* New York and London: D. Appleton-Century Co., 1936.

White, Emil, ed. *Full Color Guide to the Hearst Castle.* Big Sur: Emil White, 1958.

Whittlesey, Austin. *The Minor Ecclesiastical, Domestic and Garden Architecture of Southern Spain.* New York: Architectural Book Publishing Co., 1917.

Wilbur, Marguerite Eyer, ed. *Duflot de Mofras' Travels on the Pacific Coast.* Two volumes. Santa Ana: The Fine Arts Press, 1937.

———. *Vancouver in California 1792-1794: The Original Account of George Vancouver.* Volume II. Los Angeles: Glen Dawson, 1954.

Winslow, Carleton M., [Jr.], et al. *The Enchanted Hill: The Story of Hearst Castle at San Simeon.* Los Angeles: Rosebud Books, 1983.

Winslow, Carleton Monroe, et al. *The Architecture and the Gardens of the San Diego Exposition: A Pictorial Survey of the Panama California International Exposition.* San Francisco: Paul Elder and Company, 1916.

INDEX

Other titles from EZ Nature Books:

History of San Luis Obispo County, 1883
by Myron Angel. (Hardcover reprint, $37.50)

California's Chumash Indians
by the Santa Barbara Museum of Natural History. (Softcover, $5.95)

Santa Barbara Companion
by Tom Tuttle. A guide book. (Softcover, $8.95)

Ventura County Companion
by Tom Tuttle. A guide book. (Softcover, $8.95)

Bicycling San Luis Obispo County
by Sharon Lewis Dickerson. (Softcover, $6.95; route cards $4.95/set)

Making the Most of San Luis Obispo County
by Sharon Lewis Dickerson. A guide book. (Softcover, $9.95)

Mountain Biking the Central Coast
by Carol Berlund. (Softcover, $7.95)

Sentinels of Solitude
by Ehlers and Gibbs. Colored photos of lighthouses on the West Coast of U.S. (Softcover reprint, $14.95)

California Indian Watercraft
by Richard Cunningham. (Softcover, $12.95)

From Fingers to Finger Bowls
by Helen Linsenmeyer. A lively history of California cooking, with recipes and lore from Indian days until the turn of the century. (Softcover reprint—late 1989)

The above books may be ordered directly from the publisher, EZ Nature Books, Post Office Box 4206, San Luis Obispo, CA 93403. Please add $1.00 for the first book and 50¢ for each additional book for shipping, plus 6% sales tax for California residents.